Advance Praise for

I THOUGHT I WOULDN'T TELL IT

"Have you ever witnessed metamorphosis, the transformation of a thing into a completely different thing? Caterpillars go through a metamorphic experience to become butterflies. As a caterpillar moves to its chrysalis stage (a cocoon), it goes still.

But being still and doing nothing are not the same. The caterpillar may not move, but it's in that stillness of the chrysalis that real change happens. The wings of a beautiful, colorful butterfly emerge, and it can fly.

The transformation from caterpillar to butterfly is the best way I can describe what has happened to Deloris Dallas. The woman she was born as is not the woman she is now. The mean living she once endured is no longer her experience. She is free and creative and beautiful. She is unapologetic, having been still long enough to gain from her past the strengths that empower her future.

I have known her, have watched her, and can testify she has changed, for real."

—STEVEN HOLT
Bishop, The International Fellowship Family

"I've known Deloris for over twenty years and have had the privilege of walking alongside her during her transformation, as it were, from caterpillar to butterfly. Breaking out of the cocoon can be painful!

Many times she wanted to run away and deny the pain of her past, but God's grace has given her the strength to endure.

I want to thank her for staying with the process. I'm grateful she has allowed her history to become a chisel that has shaped her into the beautiful creation she is. She has taken flight! I pray her story will inspire others to do the same!"

—AUNDRIA HOLT
Co-Pastor of The International Fellowship Family

"Deloris Dallas has carried a heavy weight, and prayed long for relief. But beneath the story of her difficult journey is a core of love, hope, clarity, wisdom, and strength that has always guided her and inspires those of us around her now. She is an inspiration in all of our lives."

—EVELYN MCCOY
Prophetess

I THOUGHT
I WOULDN'T
TELL IT

A MEMOIR OF HARD LIFE AND HOPE

DELORIS DALLAS

abbott press®
A DIVISION OF WRITER'S DIGEST

Abbott Press books may be ordered through booksellers or by contacting:

Abbott Press
1663 Liberty Drive
Bloomington, IN 47403
www.abbottpress.com
Phone: 1-866-697-5310

Because of the dynamic nature of the Internet, any web addresses or
links contained in this book may have changed since publication and
may no longer be valid. The views expressed in this work are solely those
of the author and do not necessarily reflect the views of the publisher,
and the publisher hereby disclaims any responsibility for them.

Any people depicted in stock imagery provided by Thinkstock are models,
and such images are being used for illustrative purposes only.
Certain stock imagery © Thinkstock.

ISBN: 978-1-4582-1493-5 (sc)
ISBN: 978-1-4582-1495-9 (hc)
ISBN: 978-1-4582-1494-2 (e)

Library of Congress Control Number: 2014904723

Printed in the United States of America.

Abbott Press rev. date: 04/24/2014

Father, creator of everything,
I pray that from your unlimited resources,
you will empower me with inner strength.
Make your home in my heart,
as I trust in you.
Help love's roots grow down into me
and keep me strong,
so I can do right by my children.

Deloris Dallas

ACKNOWLEDGMENTS

As you can imagine, writing a book like this has had its ups and downs. While I'm relieved to have my story in the open, some rough memories also were resurrected. Now it's complete, for better or worse, and I have people to thank for having faith, taking time, and helping me along the way.

My family has been supportive throughout the process, for which I'm very grateful. My husband, Rupert, took me away to quiet places so I could think and write. My son, Davin, oversaw the book's cover design. My daughter, Melissa, owner and CEO of Sheeq Cosmetics, gave me a flawless makeover for the cover photograph, which was taken by Ramses Abdullah Photography.

I want to acknowledge Beverly and Timothy Leigh for their willingness to take time with me, their unflagging interest in the spirit of my story, their encouraging editorial and layout advice, and their compliments about my cooking. As we worked through this project, they became my friends.

Without the assistance of these people, and good energy from my whole community, this book would not exist. I am in their debt.

CHAPTER 1

MY JAMAICA

My Jamaica is of the senses, filled with mango, guinep, breadfruit, banana, plantain, and ackee trees, just to name a few. The air is fresh with the tang of ripening fruit and lush foliage. Wind makes the tall grasses dance, and trees wave hello to all who take time to watch. In Mount James, where I am from, my people go back and forth along a dirt road to the fields, planting, harvesting, and caring for animals. Some donkeys are ridden, but all the other animals stay in the fields at least a mile from anyone's home. Everyone prepares to sell at the market in Kingston over the weekend. There is a buzz and a sense in the districts (what we call our towns) as market days approach. Market days are a time to get dressed and I mean *really* dressed. Women wear beautiful colors of green, orange, and blue and great hair ties, and carry big, beautiful baskets. Men wear khakis and water boots. All the people gossip as they mount the truck to head for town.

Town is where things happen.

Saint Andrew Parish is located northeast of Kingston; Mount James is a beautiful rural district within it. This is where my story begins, much of it recounted to me by my grandmother, Susan, affectionately known as Mum.

Mount James is a hilly district whose sloped landscape has abundant vegetation. Up a bank, a huge mango tree grows, its roots twisting and winding in full view. The breeze picks up its leaves and carries them into the air. An older woman sits on a nearby veranda, smoking a wooden pipe. She gazes up the bank and sees her daughter, a striking twenty-one-year-old, standing there holding a baby. She is a beauty to behold, with brown skin; long, black, plaited hair; and a curvy figure. She stands next to a slender black gentleman on a big white horse with a brown spot in the center of its face. The man looks distinguished, with strong features and rich, curly hair.

But these two handsome people did not meet here on this January day to explore their love for one another or discuss their future as a family as they raise their child. No, this meeting is dark and exposes an emotional rawness as they spar to get what they want and need. The child, the purest of the three, is unaware of the impact the next moments will have on her future.

That child is me.

As Mum recalled, the two of them were arguing about something, but she wasn't sure what. As the exchange grew heated, my mother put me on the side of the road and lunged at my father, who was attempting to leave. I later learned the two were arguing about my care and financial support and about how my father did not want to help my mother. During the scuffle, I cried and squirmed and began to roll. Aunt Valsie and Mum watched with concern because there was a precipice at the road's edge. Aunt Valsie ran to catch me before I fell. Then she stood to the side as my folks continued to argue. Suddenly, my mother lifted me from my aunt's arms and shoved me at my father. He rode off, holding me, more out of frustration than anything else.

You see, Papa was a married man with children of his own. I was his indiscretion, the bastard child my mother forced him to deal with—much like he had forced my conception upon her.

My name is Deloris. I share my story, including its ugly parts, to help myself and others know the whole of my personhood, to understand why I act and think the way I do. I am not an end product; none of us are. We evolve, and my goal is to offer hope that positive change *does* come, and things *do* get better, regardless of one's beginnings. As you persevere and discover your purpose, you will become much more than those mean early circumstances might portend.

CHAPTER 2

BEGINNINGS

Unwanted from the Start

I WAS BORN TO MAVIS Aspfall and Zedekiah Barclay at 10:00 a.m. on November 27, 1949, a scorching-hot Sunday morning. They called me Deloris. Deloris Barclay. Mama was in her teens when she met my dad and twenty-one when I was born. She worked in my father's second home as his maid. In his first home, which was in the Dallas district of Saint Andrew Parish, lived his wife, four sons, and daughter. After Mama became pregnant, my father wanted nothing more to do with her, or me, and left Mama to raise me on her own. The day when she handed me to my papa, I was three months old, and a cycle of abandonment began. Mama thought she was doing her best for me, but maybe it was what was best for her as well. Her fifth-grade education limited her ability to earn and provide. In her mind, her best course was to give me away.

As Mum told me about my mother, I wondered if she'd cared that the horse could have trampled me while they argued. It seemed as though she put me by the side of the road as if I were a dead animal, to be eaten by buzzards, which in Jamaica are no joke at all. We call them John crows, and they are much bigger than American buzzards with red beaks. They come down in swarms and can devour an animal in minutes. I couldn't fathom why she hated me so much. It's taken me more than sixty years to find out.

In some ways, I draw comfort from similarities my story has with the biblical tale of Moses, but there's a difference: his life was in danger and his mother had no choice. Egyptian guards would have killed him if she hadn't let him go. So she put Moses in a basket made of papyrus straw and mud and placed him among the river bulrushes where he could be rescued. Pharaoh's daughter found him and raised him to rule Egypt. I was raised to feel insecure, threatened continuously by the sting of abandonment, and passed around during the first year of my life as Papa tried to hide my existence.

Papa on his horse that day, holding me in his arms, could have represented a tender moment between father and daughter, one that would be celebrated on family holidays and cherished in memory books. But that was the only time he ever held me or even noticed I was there.

Papa worked as a public health inspector and was respected by young and old. He was a slender, tall, handsome black man who was educated and well spoken. He resided in his second house during the workweek. He could have stashed me in that house and hired someone to care for me. After all, it was where I was conceived. But I was a bastard child, and he would not rear, parent, or love me at all. I was unwelcome in his home and life. For about six months, he pawned me off on neighbors or one or another of his girlfriends.

Then he sent me to the Jonases and a permanent home.

CHAPTER 3

I FIND A NEW FAMILY

The Jonas Clan

PERCIVAL AND MARY JONAS RAISED twenty-two children of their own in the district of Halls Delight, in the Parish of Saint Andrew, who now have kids of their own. Percival would meet my father in the town square on Friday evenings to throw back a few drinks. One day, my father got into a fight with a client who didn't like his health report on the state of the man's toilets, and Percival saved his life. His wife, Mary, had a son named Louis from another marriage, and the attack happened in front of his house. (We called him Uncle Parky because his last name was Parks.) Uncle Parky and his son, Calvin, came to my father's aid, and when Percival got wind of things, he also came to help. He took Papa home and laid him down on his own bed. Blood soaked clear through the mattress. Nobody knew whether Zedekiah Barclay was dead or alive. Percival nursed Papa back to life. On the strength of this, they became fast friends, and later, Percival agreed to take me in.

My father relinquished me, nine months old at the time, at the doorstep of the Jonases' home. Percival and Mary became my grandma and grandpa, and their children my aunts, uncles, and cousins. The younger ones played a role in my life as I grew up; the others, not so much. Some made positive impressions; others didn't. But, good or bad, they were my new family.

Grandma and Grandpa cared for me but did as they were instructed by their daughter Daisy. If they were the car, Daisy was the steering wheel. Since Percival and Mary were in their early sixties, Aunt Daisy was more of a mother figure to me; she was very strict, but kind. She made sure I was healthy and had what I needed. Every Saturday, I waited excitedly for her arrival, though I was also a little on edge because she was obsessive-compulsive, nervous and picky, and wanted everything just so. And I was sad to see her go on Monday mornings. She called me Girly, and I liked that because back then I was a girly girl. She taught me to do domestic things like cleaning house, washing clothes, and cleaning myself. She always made sure I had clothes and shoes to wear.

Aunt Daisy was in her late thirties and worked as a cook for the doctors, nurses, and other staff at a training hospital. She always brought delicious treats when she visited, and I couldn't wait to see what the surprise would be each week. Aunt Daisy never married or bore any children. Like Grandma and Grandpa, she wasn't overly affectionate; in her case, I think that was due to her upbringing and a trail of abusive men who had branded her with their cruelty. At times, I overheard her tell a friend about how badly the men in her life had treated her. I didn't completely understand what we now call verbal abuse, but I knew what she was describing wasn't right.

One of my favorite memories from that time is my Uncle Isaac's wedding. He was in his late twenties and chose me to be a flower girl. On Sundays he used to take me up to the farm in the bush to pick fruit, and he brought sandwiches and fish because fish was cheap. I was a hardworking child and felt happy and safe in his presence. That was not true of the other men in the house. As we sat and ate lunch, Uncle Isaac talked to me like a big brother. But if I did something wrong, he became a disciplinarian and bent me over his knee and spanked me. The youngest of the twenty-two children, Uncle Isaac was playful, fun, and knew how to make me laugh. He picked out nicknames just for me. They were uplifting and made me feel special. My favorite was Miss World. He called me that because I was pretty with long hair, wore nice clothes, and was clean and tidy. I guess he thought I was going places. Uncle Isaac's girlfriend was of Indian and Syrian descent and gorgeous. Her name was Jacqueline but we called her Miss J for short. She let me play with her long, silky hair and was like a big sister to me. I was honored when they invited me to be in their wedding and bought me pretty dresses. Jacqueline's family had a big house in Kingston, and I felt like a fairy princess, even though I was just a little country girl, a *pickney* as we say in Jamaica. To me, a wedding is like an outing you don't want to end. Uncle Isaac's took place at a spectacular mansion with lots of flowers. More than 250 people attended. Jacqueline had a big, beautiful family, and several children were there. We played merry-go-round and square-danced, chased butterflies, and did all the little kid things.

Grandma and Grandpa had a mentally challenged son, their firstborn. They called him Jonas, just Jonas. He was the only child, besides me, still living at home. Jonas pretty much fended for himself, and to play with him was to play with fire because he didn't know right from wrong. I kept my distance from him because there was no way to tell what he'd do, which way his wind would blow, or if he would turn into a hurricane and wipe out everyone and everything in his path. I wondered, but never asked, why he was named Jonas when that was also his last name.

Aunt Daisy called him Bobby, but she was the only person who ever called him something other than Jonas. Perhaps, with that name, he was doomed from the start. He was hard of hearing, illiterate, and almost always alone in his comings and goings. He never ate with the family and instead sat under a tree outside. Neighborhood kids seized every opportunity to tease and throw things at him, but his siblings were protective and kept him from harm. Jonas was responsible for herding the cows in at night so they could be milked, and then he took them back to the fields. I would sometimes catch him in the kitchen and watch him cook. He always shared with me. My favorite was ackee and salted fish with white flour dumpling and yellow yam. Yum. I can still taste it and see him standing there, cooking. As I got older, though, Grandma would yell to me to come out of the kitchen. I think she was concerned that Jonas, kind as he was, had no boundaries and could consider me available for sex. Did he ever ask me for sex? Yes, and he even knew enough to want to exchange shillings for it. Sometimes while being playful he would get real giggly, and I always knew to run from him when he was like that. When not doing chores he traveled the streets, visiting the houses of other family members.

The Jonases' place was not like a regular house. It was more of a hut, made of sticks, mud, and bamboo. The process of weaving sticks over and under to create the frame and walls of a house is called wattle and daub. Mud fortified with straw-like grass and water creates mortar that seals the walls, provides shelter, and keeps the house cool. The roof was made from zinc and grass. Cedar from our own trees was used to create wood floors. We were lucky to have a nice, smooth floor on which to walk; other houses had dirt floors. The rugs and mats we wiped our feet on were just old clothes or woven mats of straw. We used broom weed, plant stalks tied to a stick, to sweep the house.

We had three bedrooms and a living area that included a dining table. The beds weren't like ones you'd buy at a store, and only the adults had them. The frames were cedar, and we ripped out bulrushes from the riverbank and beat them into straw for the mattresses. I slept at the foot of Grandma and Grandpa's bed on a burlap bag stuffed with straw, using old clothes for sheets and blankets.

Our light sources were glass or brass kerosene lamps, and storm lanterns kept the wind from extinguishing the flame during hurricane weather. We also had what we called a "kitchen bitch" to use outside; it was made from a condensed milk can, a cloth wick, and oil. There was no indoor plumbing. During the day, we used an outhouse, and at night a large pot with a handle called a "chimmey." It was kept under Grandma and Grandpa's bed and used by everyone. Nobody went to the outhouse at night because of the cockroaches and bullfrogs. During the day, we used a lit newspaper to singe around the edge of the toilet so they would go away, then dropped the newspaper into the pit. At night, everyone used the same pot and hoped it wouldn't fill up. In the morning, I'd take it to the outhouse and empty it. Then I washed the pot, turned it over to dry, and brought it back into the house at night. As a child, I had chores I had to do, and this was one of them. (The last time I saw one of those pots was in Leavenworth, Washington, while I was on vacation. People were popping corn in it, and my son said, "Mom, they're using a pisspot to make popcorn!")

This is how we lived; this was my normal. Even cleaning the chimmey was normal, as disgusting as that seems to me now.

My father, Zedekiah, paid periodic visits to our home. I'd watch him go into a room with Grandpa, where they would talk for what seemed like hours. No one kept secret the fact he was my father, though he never asked to see me. During each visit,

I'd fantasize that he would hoist me up to the back of his horse and take me with him—only this time he would keep me, and love me, and care for me like a father should. Distraught with disappointment each time he left without me, I was a little girl who wanted nothing more than to make her father proud. I'd asked about my mother, but no one wanted to talk about her, except to say that she'd died when I was a baby and I should forget about her. So all my hopes hinged on the actions of my father. During his long visits with Grandpa, I wondered what I could do to make him want me. I longed to write a storybook ending, but I was a princess in a tower with no Prince Charming in sight. I can still see him riding away on his beautiful white horse with the brown spot on its forehead, looking so dashing, as I stood with tears in my eyes and the bitterness of hopes dashed hardening my heart. Eventually, I stopped looking for him, and he stopped coming.

CHAPTER 4

SEVEN YEARS LATER

Life in Our House

WE BUILT A NEW HOUSE when I was seven. The old place was converted into a butchery, where we smoked and hung meats and stored food like grains, corn, beans, and peas for the coming year. When I helped with the cooking, I would go over—it was right across the veranda—and cut off different parts of the meat depending on what was needed for the dish.

The new house was built from steel and cement blocks. The veranda, though, was cement tile, colored red and then polished, which was one of my chores. I'd light a wax block, hold it over a brush made of dried coconut husk, and let the wax drip into it. Then I'd rub that into the floor, always working toward the door. I had a rag under my knees to buff up the wax as I moved. At the end of the veranda, I would stand on the rag and scoot around with it under my feet to enhance the shine.

There were three bedrooms and a dining/living room with a built-in cabinet for Granny's special dishes. The dining-room table and Granny's dishes, which we called crockery (not china), were reserved for important occasions, and oh did the food taste good when we ate on them! I couldn't get enough of that good taste in my mouth and just wanted to keep eating. Grandpa made our table, three chairs, and a bench from cedar and stained them a beautiful deep cherry color. I'm not sure why he didn't stain the built-in dish cabinet to match the rest; maybe he didn't notice the difference. At any rate, they were well built and solid.

None of us had a lot of clothes, so large closets weren't necessary. Grandma packed any new or nice clothes, sheets, towels, and pillowcases in trunks. The bedrooms were small, about half the size of a standard American bedroom. Nothing went to waste; even Grandpa's old shirts were used as either extra stuffing for my bed or as mats for wiping feet at the door.

Granny was particular about her crockery, so we had to clean everything immediately after we ate. And we didn't use dishrags. We'd pick leaves from the susumba plant, make a pan of dishwater, and use brown soap. Something in the susumba leaves made the dishes sparkle better than any cleaning product off the grocery shelves.

As I said, the crockery came out only on festive occasions, when people like my grandpa's brother, Uncle Claude, and Aunt Liz from Kingston (they were originally from Panama), would visit. Aunt Liz was something, with her yellow skin and long hair. She let me take her hair down, play in it, pull gray hairs out, and scratch the dandruff, which smelled sweaty. She looked forward to this process like therapy. I looked forward to it because it made me feel appreciated and loved. She always brought a treat and never came empty-handed. They visited us every Sunday. They came early for breakfast, and Grandpa and his brother would talk. Granny would cook all day, and I would play in Aunt Liz's long, thick hair for hours, parting through every strand and picking gray hair. They didn't go to church, so there was nothing else to do.

13

Granny was a pretty woman of Portuguese, English, and Jamaican descent, with beautiful black hair that framed her white complexion. All my kindness and generosity comes from her. She rose at 4:00 a.m. every day to cook breakfast for the whole family and also all the wives and husbands who passed by on their way to work. They would stop for a johnnycake and salt fish and to fill their thermoses with coffee or hot chocolate. Granny roasted coffee beans over a fire and then used a big stick, similar to a pestle, to grind them in a mortar, and then bag the grounds for future use. She always knew just how much to put in the big open pot on the stove to accommodate the gallons of brew she'd need for her guests. She'd steep the grounds in the water, then strain them and sweeten the pot with sugar and fresh cow's milk. By 6:00 a.m. she was back in bed and up again at seven thirty to see me off to school, about the same time her grandkids would start rolling in for her to babysit. In my eyes, Granny was perfect. I wish I could say the same for Grandpa.

CHAPTER 5

I LEARN TO GROW THINGS

Grandpa's Dark Side

GRANDPA HAD MOMENTS OF EXTREME kindness, and I am grateful that he took me in when no one else would. His family harvested their food from the land. Grandpa always shared what he had with me; for example, he gave me the first milk from the cow's udder—the best tasting thing ever. But love was displayed in his house through action, not touch. We did not share hugs, and I did not sit on Grandma's lap as she read me stories. Yet I know I was cared for.

Grandpa was a ranger at Hope Botanical Garden and Zoo and a teacher of the outdoors. When I was quite young, he taught me to shoot a rifle. He'd take me bird hunting. I got to pick up the birds, put them in a bag, pluck their feathers, and clean them when we got home. He taught me how to roast birds on a fire. I was raised to work hard for what I wanted and not depend on other people to give me anything. Jamaica doesn't have a welfare system like America does. Orphans received assistance, but poor

15

families did not, so we relied on the resources of the land and the fruits of our labor. Grandpa taught me how to plant things in the ground too, which is where I got my green thumb. Today, people stop their cars to look at my house and garden; they even go so far as to take pictures and knock on my door and ask questions.

I learned how to create one tree that yielded three different fruits, a technique called in-grafting. Grandpa showed me how to cut a healthy stem from an orange tree with a special knife, bring in stems from two other types of trees, and use a kind of tape to keep them together on the host tree's branch. Sometimes, it didn't catch, because it dried up, but I never saw Grandpa do one that didn't catch. In-grafting was more successful with the same species of fruit because it took less energy, but any fruit would work. The result was always something unusual and great, as each fruit adopted characteristics from the others. The only tree you couldn't in-graft was banana because of its big trunk. We could in-graft different kinds of avocados, a multitude of fruits, even roses. Country people didn't have roses, though. Instead, beautiful wild flowers grew rampant, and we just picked what we wanted or dug up ferns that grew by the rivers and replanted them in our yard. I enjoyed being in nature, surrounded by beautiful flowers, plants, and trees. They made my life happier.

Every spring, we planted vegetables, and I eagerly anticipated their growth. Grandpa dug a mound to grow yellow, white, and purple yams, and I had my own spot to dig. I cut his potato vines and poked them in the ground, assuming I wasn't doing it right and that nothing would ever grow. You put something in the ground, but you don't know what will come out. You have to trust in nature. And I did.

When it was time to reap the sweet potatoes, I dug mine up and there were eight or nine gigantic ones. Grandpa told me, "You do good," and I said, "Me can do better if you keep teachin' me." If Grandpa was planting his peas and beans, I'd be in my garden planting peas and beans. The only thing I didn't like was moving rocks because I never knew what was under them, and I didn't like creepy crawlers. Occasionally, we'd take a break and snack on johnnycakes and sugar water (lemonade). He trusted me with his cigars, which he made himself from tobacco he planted. He'd pull the leaves from the plant and hang them in the smoke house to cure. Then he'd take the dried leaves to his little table, pull the veins from the tobacco, and roll them into cigars. When he finished, he called me to light his cigar for him. Every child would like to taste tobacco, pull a stick from the fire, and puff on a cigar until it was lit. I did that just about every day, although I never inhaled, because it didn't smell good. I loved it when he told me to do that because it meant he trusted me.

When he wanted a drink, he sent me to buy his rum, writing his order on a piece of paper and folding it up with the money so that it couldn't fall out and get lost. The paper went in a bag that I'd give to the clerk. He'd remove the money from the paper, put my purchase in the bag with any change, and I was on my way again.

The abuse from my Grandpa started when I was about eleven. The first time, he hit me in the face with the back of his hand. Granny went to the market on weekends, and I always went with her to sell produce that we'd picked earlier. Again, everyone looked forward to market days. We would harvest fruit and vegetables on Wednesday. Some may have been from the week before, set aside to fully ripen. Only the best went to the market. On Fridays, I stayed home from school to help carry things, and Grandpa took the day off from work with the intention of accompanying Granny. Instead, he and his colleagues went to the rum bar and drank.

This was a weekly ritual. We'd come home from market, and he would return home late and demand that we prepare food at one in the morning. He would swear and wake me up to heat his food, and Grandma would say, "No, he should have come earlier to eat with the family." On one occasion, he grabbed me by the hand. Granny pushed him off and got between us, but he went around her and slapped me with the palm of his big hand with long fingers. As any child would, I started screaming, and they started arguing. He went in his room, grabbed his gun, and said he would kill us all. I thought he really would kill us, since he was a man who shot well and didn't miss. I said my good-byes.

Because he was drunk, he had a hard time opening the breech to load the bullets. Granny pushed me behind her and used her full force to shove him out of the way. He fell to the floor, and she grabbed the gun from him. (She was a force when she was angry.) He passed out, and we left him there. That was the first time I had seen this side of him, but it wouldn't be the last.

When we went back into the room, I didn't feel scared anymore, because Granny knew he wouldn't get up, and she was not cowed by his bad behavior. We both went to bed. If anything more happened, I felt Grandpa would go after her, not me, and I knew Granny could hold her own.

From then on, that was his habit: if I did something wrong or didn't do something he wanted, he would slap me in the face. Granny told him, "You're going to make the *pickney* grow up deaf." If she was not close enough to stop him, she would yell at him to draw his attention away from me or run interference as best she could.

The First Really Bad Time

Grandpa started to touch me in places he had no business touching and threatened me so I would not tell. The first time he tried to rape me, we were all up late cleaning naseberries with buckets of water and rags. We'd wipe sap and dust from the outsides, and then leave them to ripen in baskets to get ready for market. Naseberries couldn't be picked when ripe as they were too soft to clean properly. So we picked them when they were green, cleaned them, and let them ripen in baskets.

We all were tired, so Granny and I went to bed. Remember, my bed was at the foot of hers, on the floor. Grandpa got up to use the chimmey. I was lying down on my mattress pad, sleeping, and Grandpa came over and lay on top of me. I was on my stomach; he was on my back. That is a horrible feeling for a child, I'll tell you. He reached in his pants and pulled out what he had in there. That thing was cold like a slug and lifeless; the more he tried to get in between my legs, the more I scrunched up. I was about to scream, but he put his hand over my mouth. He kept trying but nothing happened. His thing was worn out and dead from the alcohol; plus, he was in his sixties. Finally, he gave up and crawled off, acting like he was using the chimmey again. Then he went back and lay down. In the morning, he told me that if I didn't have sex with him I would suffer bad luck the rest of my life and never amount to anything. But if I did, I would get what I wanted, and everything would turn to gold. I was a child and didn't know what to think. *Is this normal? Is this happening to anyone else?*

Uncle Stanford had gotten fresh with me before, but this was first time for Grandpa. I do believe he thought his son was already messing with me, and I was having sex at a young age because he'd ask me if boys touched me or if I took my clothes off for boys. Then there was the way he looked at me, even when we went bird hunting. I'd have dress on and would not be conscious of the way I was sitting; my panties would show, and he would stare. I'd understand then and shift positions. One time I bent over, and he touched me. He said, "Don't bend over like that." He told me he was trying to teach me a lesson, but I believe he was just seeing how much I'd put up with.

Otherwise, there was no hugging or kissing, because that was not my family's way. I don't know if other families got that, but I did not. I didn't long for that kind of innocent affection either, because I never saw it expressed by the families and people I knew. Most of them were closed, mean-spirited, and didn't show love. I thought that was normal.

After receiving those unwanted sexual advances at such an early age, I developed a callous heart. I felt, *if this is what the rest of my life will be like, I need to fortify myself.* I realized anything done behind closed doors was probably wrong. What happened to me never took place in the presence of anyone else. And the beatings happened because I never gave in. In time, I became mean and angry—like them in a way—in order to fight them.

I wasn't taught to be nice or friendly. I didn't grow up to be a sweet little girl whose mom and dad would hug her and who would run between them to get some love. No, I stood far off and listened to the fighting.

I never saw cuddling. I used to spy on Aunt Icy because I wanted to know what Uncle Stanford and Grandpa were after. I'd peek in when her lover visited. He'd drop his pants and get in the bed. I never heard laughter or "honey" or giggling, just the bedsprings squeaking up and down. Then he'd get up, wipe off, and leave, like he didn't care at all. It seemed to me that dogs had more fun.

I heard love songs once in a while, but couldn't understand when Engelbert Humperdinck sang, "You want to get close to me." I didn't know what you did when you got close to someone. I never wanted to be with a man, because I thought it was gross.

I got drunk once when I was twelve. It was at a party hosted by Isaac, one of my favorite uncles. Every Wednesday after work he invited friends over to the house to cook and eat. He kept some ducks in a handy pen and would kill some, and we'd clean, pluck, and season them. I never ate any, because I couldn't stand the big old webbed feet and beak—looked like buzzard to me.

They used Kool-Aid, red syrup, and lime to make rum punch, and while the grownups ate duck, I drank rum punch. It was exhilarating to sneak something, knowing I could be caught any moment. But I didn't understand how bad it could get or that it was something I shouldn't overdo, so I kept drinking like it was normal Kool-Aid. After a while, I couldn't even taste the rum. I found out, though, when I tried to walk to the bedroom, that the effects were considerable. I was woozy. I felt like I were walking on air. I made it to the bed and slept, but woke up the next morning covered in red vomit. I could have choked on the vomit and died. Or I could have died from alcohol poisoning. That was an early lesson. I did get a spanking, but only because I took the rum punch without asking. Uncle Isaac said he would have given some to me, but not too much. He disciplined me so I would learn never to take things that weren't mine.

The day after the party, he bought me a flowered dress, ribbons for my hair, and nice socks. He wrapped them up in paper. It wasn't a peace offering for the spanking; it was thanks for helping with his party. He always brought me little gifts of two shillings and sixpence, which would be like an American quarter. It was not much, but it was enough to buy treats at the corner store up the street. My favorites were peppermint balls—great big ones—or peppermint sticks. There were also bags of cocktion, which is like caramel corn but with red and green colors on each piece. Paradise plum was a hard candy sprinkled with sugar; its green, red, purple, and yellow colors made it so pretty, children had to buy it. Sometimes if I had money left over, I'd buy a snow cone. Some kids ate all their candy as soon as they bought it, but I liked to savor mine. I would hide it; then late at night when everyone else was in bed, I'd pull it out and eat. Kids are kids, and grownups don't need to know everything we have. Our secrets are all we really have to hold onto, I found that out at a very young age.

CHAPTER 6

FENDING FOR OURSELVES

Living without Appliances

WE DIDN'T HAVE MODERN TOOLS, for the most part. We usually did things by hand. To take a bath, for instance, I'd fetch water from the river and put it in the sun to warm. We'd use the stove in the kitchen to heat it some more, then cool it with cold water. When I was small, I was bathed in a wash pan and that was the best bath I ever had, one of a kind. Later, the children would fit into a galvanized tub, in which adults would wash our hair and bathe us because they didn't think we could clean ourselves properly. That lasted until we were ten or so. And, as we grew up, we just put a board down, stood on it, splashed water on ourselves with a small pan, soaped down, and rinsed. I loved using Cashmere Bouquet bath soap because it smelled so sweet and nice. But we also had antiseptic carbolic soap, like doctors use in hospitals before they go to surgery. There was never a worry about me taking baths, because I loved the water and a good scrub; I usually just wanted to take a nap after that. Our skin never dried out when we used river water and the good-smelling soap. When it was really hot, we could wash in the river, but only older girls did that because they could throw rocks or yell to fend off men who'd wander by.

Granny taught me to wash clothes on a washboard, using a brush or corncob and a bar of brown soap. I still remember the smell of fresh laundry hanging on the line to dry. It smelled better than any of today's fabric softeners, and the clothes were cleaner too. We didn't buy bleach from the store. Granny spread the white clothes out on rocks and kept wetting them. The sun bleached the stains out.

Granny also made her own starch from yucca she'd peel, grate, juice, and then put in a pan of water to settle. When the sediment that developed on the bottom dried in the sun, it became a white powder. She starched just about everything, even our bloomers! Granny poured boiling water over the white powder and mixed it until it became this gluey mess, which cooled into a jelly. Then she put the jelly into another basin of water and dropped in the clothes to starch them. The final step was to wring out the clothes and hang them on the line to dry. Result: stiff clothes.

We set aside separate days for washing and ironing. To prepare for ironing, we'd fill a bowl with water, and take the dry, starched clothes from the line. Then, draping an article across our laps, we'd sprinkle water on it, fold it, roll it tight, and put it into a basket, working on one piece at a time until the laundry was done. To avoid water spots, the water needed to soak into the clothes, so we let them sit in a towel-covered basket for about an hour. Meanwhile, we built a wood fire to heat the irons, for a time. Once they were hot, we rubbed them in dirt to remove black soot and used banana leaves to cool them down; then we wiped them down with wet rags to make doubly sure our whites didn't get any black spots.

Granny taught me how to give and share and that food was a good way to make friends. Everyone likes to eat, and when you share food it shows you care. Truth was that no man would want you if you couldn't cook because there were no microwaves or fast food. Granny could cook, and she was more than happy to teach me everything she knew.

We didn't have a refrigerator, when we killed a pig or goat or whatever, we stored the meat in a smoke house and cut off what we needed for each meal. My favorite foods were stew peas and rice with pig's tail and salted beef; fried herring sprat; and fricassee chicken cooked in hot oil with onion, garlic, spices, butter, seasonings, and sugar until it was brown and crisp. It was the best chicken I ever had. I liked everything Granny cooked. She made fresh juices too—carrot juice with ginger or milk, or soursop juice taken from really ripe fruit of the same name, which makes a refreshing drink when cow's milk is added to it.

When I wasn't doing chores or in school, I played house by myself. I even made my own dolls, using unraveled burlap-sack pieces and roots from the grass that grew by the riverbank for hair. Barbie dolls were not in abundance, but creativity was. Sometimes I'd pretend I was the mommy, taking care of my little girl, baking cookies and candies like Granny. At other times I pretended I was the little girl, living in my daddy's house and playing with lots of other children. This pretend life was of course my deepest wish and desire, what I truly longed for. I was happy with my pretending, but I knew that huge pieces of my life were missing.

Halls Delight Social Life

Granny loved to look after everyone else, but she didn't like to go out much, except when Grandpa took us all to a quadrille (square dancing), our national dance. Granny lit up the floor with her dancing. Uncle Isaac and the whole family could dance, so they'd all come, if they could. We'd get to the dance about 8:00 or 9:00 p.m. and dance until 1:00 a.m. There was always plenty of food, drink, and Jamaican soda pop. My favorites were cream soda and cola champagne, which tasted just like the real thing. It truly was an unusual treat because we didn't often get it at home.

A community band of self-taught musicians called out different moves as they played their instruments—sax, trumpet, bass guitar, banjo, drum, even a big grater. They also had homemade instruments made from found things. I loved getting dressed up in my square-dancing attire. The women and girls wore white blouses with embroidery on the sleeves and embroidered designs—like a donkey, Doctor Bird (our national bird) or hibiscus flowers—on the front. We tied our heads with colorful bands, and our shoes looked like tap shoes. Sewn under our skirts was stiffly starched tulle, what we called crinoline, which made our skirts stand straight out and twirl big as we danced.

Sometimes young people would take over the floor, while the adults sat on the sidelines, cheering us on. Fortunately, I'd learned the quadrille in school, so when we went to the dances I was ready to cut the rug with the best. I also learned the maypole, merengue, and others. As I got older, I often won dance contests. Whenever I found out we were going to a dance, I got very excited. It was fun to meet kids I usually didn't hang out with and see kids from school, even ones I didn't like. They acted differently when their parents were with them and lost the urge to talk bad about others, afraid of being overheard. Everyone forgot about all the bad stuff because when we were out on that dance floor, we hadn't a care in the world.

My childhood best friend, a girl named May, got pregnant at the age of eleven; the father was a neighborhood boy much older than she was. We didn't live far from each other and seemed to have a similar home life, except she had real parents (although they fought all the time, using knives and anything else at hand).

In fact, I remember when she got her first period because I told her she was bleeding when she stood up in class. May taught me girls could get pregnant at a young age, and I wanted to stay the hell away from men because I did not want that happening to me.

She also tried to show me how to be a lesbian, well "to love" is how she described it. We both had skipped school in the afternoon and were walking down by the river on the way home. We stopped and began to talk about what life would be like when we grew up.

We both wanted to love and be loved. I told her how Grandpa had been touching me; that's what you do with best friends, tell them everything. She seemed to understand and decided she would help me with my quest for love. So she made a bed of grass in the bushes, and we both lay down and continued to talk. She got me to undress as we were talking. She said she would hug me and show me "how to love." Then she rolled on top of me. I asked her what she was doing. She said, "Remember, I said I'd show you how to love without getting pregnant." I told her no thanks, she had to get up, that was nasty and making me sick. At the time, I was thinking about Grandpa, who had something to connect with, and wondering how two girls would. She didn't know either. Even though we both felt bad about our lives and she was just looking for love, I told her to stay away from me. I was not having it. Later May found a boyfriend named Cheva. She told me she was crazy in love with him, this older boy, that he made her feel all she was missing. Whatever May was doing with Cheva, she enjoyed. Eventually, she bore more children and aged faster than her chronological years.

I loved my friend dearly as a confidant and fun-buddy, but she could not give me what I longed for: the acceptance, encouragement, and love of a parent.

I didn't have a boyfriend and didn't want one. A kid named Caleb was about the same age as May and I were. He was such a pest. Once we were playing in the river while washing clothes, and he tried to hold me down. I fought him off, pushed him hard, and tossed a rock at him, so he ran away. I told him to come back tomorrow and we'd play some more, just to get rid of him. After he left, I went back to the river, dug a hole in the sand and left it overnight. The next day, I told him to get into the hole so I could see how tall he was, and I buried him up to his neck in dirt. Then May came by, saw what I'd done, and called Caleb a fool, saying, "You're going to get buried alive." But he thought it was funny.

Days came and went, and still he messed with me. You see, each time we washed clothes, we'd take our own off to wash them too. We were digging this big pond, and Caleb took off his clothes to help, but then hit his penis on our legs intentionally. May told him, "I'm going to castrate you." We had a tin can lid with sharp edges. May held him down and pulled his foreskin up as though to circumcise, and she made me slice him. Oh, did it bleed! We panicked and tore rags and tied it up. That was the last time Caleb ever bothered us.

CHAPTER 7

AUNTS AND UNCLES

The Jonas Children

I DON'T REMEMBER ALL OF the Jonas children, my adoptive aunts and uncles, as they were grown with their own lives when I came onto the scene. A few, however, left impressions on me.

Aunt Daisy, as I've mentioned already, was my primary caretaker.

Aunt Ivy was one of the younger Jonas kids; she was married with a son and two daughters, Pansy (or Miss P) and Viv. Pansy was five years my senior; as we got older we lost touch until I found her again in 2003. Aunt Ivy was known for being strict, which Pansy often experienced as she would get a beating at the drop of a hat. When Aunt Ivy found out that seventeen-year-old Pansy was pregnant, for instance, she tied her daughter to a mango tree with an ant's nest at its base. She called for someone to bring her a stick and used it to beat Pansy, even though she was pregnant. Aunt Ivy worked at the hospital and on the side was a dressmaker who did garment alterations.

Aunt Icy was a hateful one; and she suffered a horrible death. She was shot point-blank in her own yard. Let me tell you about her. During my childhood, Icy had a split personality. Sometimes she was really nice and took me to the dance with her and her boyfriend. They'd bring me food and soda pop, and the music was nice and loud. We had a long walk home but didn't care because the dance was so much fun. Icy watched to make sure no one messed with me. As time went on, though, I came to realize Icy was a vindictive person. Perhaps she had me accompany her to the dances so she didn't have to walk home alone. She was very selfish. She only did what benefited her. She had three kids with three different fathers. I am the godmother of one of her daughters, Elaine the baby. I felt she needed a big sister in her life, and because the other two kids, Carroll the eldest and Tamara in the middle, didn't have the ability to be big sisters. In fact, Tamara bore a child herself when she was only eleven. Many times I had to shield Elaine from danger because she was nearly raped by the man Icy brought for her oldest daughter. Aunt Icy was like the woman of Samaria, having many men but none of her own.

Aunt Eva was abusive towards me, so much so that Aunt Daisy would argue with her about the way she beat me silly. She was an unhappy woman married to an abusive man and had two bratty kids. They weren't good parents at all. As I think about her actions, they seem bipolar because she didn't like me yet would say I could come to her house for lunch. Then she'd reverse course again and accuse me of stealing from her. She was like a cow that gives you a bucket of milk, then kicks it over.

Uncle Stanford was another abusive soul. I lived in his house briefly when I was an adult and heard him beat his wife until she screamed. When I was little, he tried to take me to the bushes and pull my underwear off, but somehow I always got away. I still have marks on my body from beatings he gave me with his thick cowhide belt. He would pull off that belt and use it on me—I was between eight and twelve years old and very skinny, and he was around 250 pounds—and then order me to the bush to pick mangoes, where he'd chase and try to rape me. One time I was very lucky; there were people around when I screamed, and a man asked if everything was okay. Stanford lied and said I was afraid of a lizard. Please, I grew up playing with lizards.

The only other Jonas children I remember are Uncle George and Uncle William, who were very quiet. I was never close to them as they were older and averse to taking on any mentoring role with me. Most of them seemed to not like me because I wasn't a Jonas; I had no identity in the family. They considered me a bother, a bad kid. They had no understanding of what I was going through as an orphan and the victim of others' depravity.

CHAPTER 8

MY MOTHER REAPPEARS

Stolen Away from the Jonases

IT WAS THE SUMMER OF 1962, and I was thirteen years old when my life with Grandma and Grandpa Jonas came crashing down around me. My mother, whom I'd never known and had long been told was dead, suddenly appeared. Oh, there just are no words for the confusion, shock, and upset I felt. What was up became down, and what was down became up.

It was a Friday, a different sort of Friday because I was at school. As I've said, Friday was market day, and I usually spent it with Grandma, dressed up and ready to smile at people so we'd sell all we had. This particular Friday I was at school because it was Home Economics Day, a great interest of mine, and the teachers wanted to show off my skills. The plan was for me to bake and cook, as that was part of the class curriculum. I got into the kitchen around 10:00 a.m. and was preparing to start my project when I was called to the office. This surprised me because it had never happened before. The only explanation was that something was wrong or someone was hurt. At first, I didn't respond, because

I thought it was a prank. Then I was called again and this time was told my grandmother was ill. I stopped what I was doing immediately and reported to the office, where I found a man and woman I didn't know. The woman said, "Mrs. Jonas sent us to get you because she got sick at the market and needs to go home." I believed them because Granny was an old lady. And the fact they were driving made sense because I usually walked from school to my granny's, and it took forty minutes. Driving would make for a much quicker trip, what you'd expect in an emergency.

How deceptive they were! In those days, anyone could pick a child up from school as long as they knew the child's name and family's name, so the principal let me go with them. As we exited through the school gate, I still didn't know who they were. They escorted me to a car and told me to get in so they could take me to my grandmother who was waiting at the market. I noticed right away the car was heading in a strange direction. I yelled out, "Where are you taking me? You are going the wrong way!" I began to cry, but they just drove on. I screamed at the top of my lungs, but no one paid any attention. I tried to open the door but couldn't do it. Then the woman scolded me. "Stop crying. I am your mother, and I am taking you home to my house." I said, "You are lying to me. My mother is dead. I don't have a mother. I've never seen you before." I wailed on, explaining that I only had Grandma and Grandpa. I begged them to take me back, sobbing that Granny was waiting and would be looking for me. "Please, please, please," I cried.

By then, though, we were in neighborhoods I didn't recognize. I was scared they were going to kill me. Finally, we stopped at a place called Stony Hill. The woman, her man, and the driver got out of the car. They went into a bar to eat and left me alone outside. It struck me that if I got out of the car and announced I'd been kidnapped, no one would believe me as people didn't purposely take on children. They had enough trouble taking care of their own. More likely, someone would ask, "Child, are you hungry?" and bring me some food. The best thing to do was sit tight and wait. Plus, I was terrified I'd come to harm, and I had no idea where I was. I knew no one, and expected a reaction like, "Straighten up, and wait for your parents to come to you." Nobody talked about kidnapping in those days. They might ask, "Who did you come with?" And I'd tell them. Then they'd go inside and say a child outside was having a fit.

A while later, the woman came out to the car and asked, "Are you hungry?" and before I could answer, she gave me the crust of a Jamaican patty that she had bought in the bar. (Patties are meat pies folded over like a calzone; they are so good with their seasoned meat, veggies, and flaky flour crust.) After I ate the crust and finished the woman's cream soda, she went back to join her man and the driver at the bar. In about an hour, they all returned to the car, bringing me another half-eaten patty. Some people threw away the crust because the meat filled them up. Imagine how I felt, knowing how the patty was supposed to taste but instead eating only a crust that had been chewed by someone else. The driver started the car, and away we went.

As we traveled along, my heart began to pound with fright. The three of them asked me, "What do you do at Grandma and Grandpa's?" "What kind of chores they give you to do?" "How bright are you in school?" I fired back answers. I described my life as happy, let them know how much I was loved, and begged them to take me home. The person who called herself my mother screamed at me in a harsh voice. "You'll go back over my dead body. I am not taking you back!" She went on, "I am your mother. I gave birth to you on a hot Sunday morning, November 27, 1949, on your Grandmother Susan's bed. I breastfed you three months." There was a pause as her man whispered something to her, and then everything became silent; you could have heard a pin drop.

My Mother's House

There was no more conversation at all until we reached a place called Mount Friendship. The woman pointed up a hill and said, "Your father lives up there." I couldn't see his house but was able to spot a landmark without anyone knowing I did. We continued on for about three miles. Then the car stopped, and everyone got out. "This is my home," she said and pointed to the other side of the road. I saw a beautiful white house trimmed with blue and some red. It looked like a two-story house from afar, but when I got closer, I could see the back was built on beams, giving it an under-cellar where small animals could sleep, chickens could lay eggs, and dogs and cats could bear their young ones. A little feeling of relief came over me because I thought I might have my own room and bed and just maybe I could be happy and grow to love her and her man—who would now be my stepfather and hadn't spoken a word to me since he'd laid eyes on me at my school. The only thing I'd heard coming from his mouth all day was vague mumbling and loud laughter. Every now and then, he'd smoke a cigarette and spit out the car window.

We entered the house; the interior seemed beautiful, well-furnished, and clean, but I sensed that little love was shared there. The place had a cold, frightening feeling. I looked around to see where my bed was, but didn't find one. By now, it was nearing nighttime, too. I had no change of clothes, only the ones on my back, and I was scared to ask what I would sleep in and where I would sleep. Before I could voice these concerns, though, my mother said, "Here is one of my old dresses ... sleep in it!" She gave me some other old clothes to make a paddle (sleeping place) on the floor. I prayed to God for morning to come so I could run back to my home with Granny, the only home I'd known for thirteen years.

Daylight broke, but I didn't know in which direction to go, so I waited until everyone woke up, and then she gave me chores to do. I still had no clothes, except the ones in which she'd stolen me away and the old dress in which I'd slept. She gave me a needle, thread, and scissors so I could cut down another of her dresses and make my own panty and dress so I could have a change of clothes. Luckily, I had learned how to sew in home economics. My mother only knew what the school had told her—that I excelled in home economics and could sew and cook—so she figured I could make my own clothes. She gave me a needle, thread, and some of her old clothes, and I made a dress. For a while, that was the only dress I had. Every day, I had to wash it so I'd have something clean to put on next day.

When it was time to take a bath, I had to fetch water from a pipe across the road because there was no running water at the house. We used a bucket to catch the water, then poured it into a big wooden bath barrel. This was done every day and, after a while, I got used to fetching water in the morning, placing it in a basin, and bathing outside in the open, although it may have been wiser to do it at night when no one could see me. That was how I spent the first three days living with my mother and her man—and later my stepbrother, whom she treated like a king. My stepbrother was polite, but like his father he said little. He had his own room with a bed and some small furniture. He seemed happy to me. He and his dad left early in the morning and were gone all day. In the evening, they came home with food from the field and wood to cook with.

On day four, my mother and her man got dressed and left on public transportation. I didn't know where they went, so I cleaned the house, fed the fowl and pigs, and swept the yard until they returned. Others lived there—a teacher rented a room on the side of the house—but I hadn't met them yet. I hadn't even seen anyone else. Since I wasn't allowed inside, except when time came to clean or when she and her man were away, I was not allowed to visit with the people that live there. My best friends were the animals. The back of the house was on stilts, so there was a lot of space under there. The chickens went way up in back to lay eggs; the pigs and dogs roamed around. A little wooden bench was attached to the wall. That was my space. I would sit there to eat. Well, sort of, because if I didn't stand up, the animals would try to get my food, causing the chickens to flutter their wings and raise a lot of dust.

The adults returned around 4:00 p.m. and told me they had purchased clothes for me (hallelujah!) so I could go to school. I was thankful for the new underwear and brown crepe-soled shoes, but apprehensive as well, not knowing what was waiting for me.

Living in Hell on Earth

Monday morning dawned, and my mother took me to the neighborhood school, Mount James All-Age School, where students attended from preschool to high school. As I walked in, kids began to laugh. At first, I thought they weren't laughing at me—I was a beautiful young lady, with a full head of long hair, so they couldn't be laughing at me. But after my mother registered me and left, and I was introduced to the class, they began to laugh again. They were making fun of my damned brown crepe-soled shoes, which they called "brown pus!" Apparently, the boys wore brown crepe soles. Girls wore *white* crepe soles. I was embarrassed to tears and angry. But my mom wouldn't change my shoes, because she thought the white would get dirty too easily. She didn't know how carefully I kept my clothes and that cleaning my shoes would not have troubled me. The teacher finally stepped in and told the kids to stop taunting me, reminding some they were not wearing shoes at all. She let them know you can only wear what your parents buy for you. It was a searing, depressing experience for me, and I became a different child after that, quiet and withdrawn. My only comfort was my belief that God loved me and would help me through.

After school, I did all my chores before nightfall because I hated the dark. We didn't have electricity, so our light came from kerosene lamps. I sat in the cellar to do my homework since I wasn't allowed inside until it was time for bed. I also had to be very quiet, or my mother would slap me or call me names. Before long, I grew to be afraid of her, never knowing what she'd do next. Her real personality emerged, and she terrorized my life.

On Friday mornings, I had to wake up at 4:00 a.m., rain or shine, to walk with my stepbrother four miles up a steep hill to the field and help bring produce back to the house, which then would be packed up for market. Sometimes I had to make the trek up the hill myself to take breakfast to her man and my stepbrother as they harvested the produce. It was frightening to walk alone by myself at that hour. I remember on several occasions passing by a place called Belmore Hill, where a bull had been tied so it could graze on grass. I walked toward the bull because he was in my path, and he came at me with a fierce look and evil intent. Thank God he was moored with a big strong rope to a big strong tree; when he lunged at me the rope held him back. Otherwise, the food I was carrying would have been ruined, and I would have been dead. I was able to run away with the food on my head. When I finally reached where they were and delivered their breakfast, they questioned why I was late. I explained what had happened. They didn't believe me and said the bull wouldn't hurt me. To add insult to injury, they loaded a basket with yams for me to put on my head and take back the same way, again by myself. This time I rebelled. I told them they would have to kill me because I wasn't going by that bull again. I knew I'd be in trouble with my mother, but that was a chance I was willing to take. I waited until they were finished, and we left together. On the way back, sure enough, the bull came lunging at us. It was unnerving, and it provoked colorful language from them, but I felt vindicated because now they believed me.

We all made it back home safely. After packing the produce, my mother dressed and proceeded to her place at the market. The next morning, after a full day of selling, she returned home on the market truck. While she was gone, I had to fetch water to fill the water barrel, sweep the yard, and clean the house.

Cleaning

Cleaning a house in Jamaica was a different from cleaning one in the United States. There was no vacuum cleaner, so everything was done manually. The house floors were wood, so on Saturdays I dyed them with bark water (which imparted a mahogany color) or straw dye (red powder that was mixed in water). Once the floors were dry, I waxed them with a brush made out of coconut husks, like I did the Jonases' veranda, then followed each application with a soft cloth to buff up the shine. My finished floors were like mirrors; I could see my face in them.

Many Saturdays, my mother would return home and beat me if one speck of dirt or footprint remained. My backside would pay with whatever she had in her hands. And as she unpacked her market basket, she gave treats to my stepbrother and whoever else had helped her. I can't remember ever getting any of those.

For Saturday dinner, my mother cooked her favorites, which included steamed goatfish with yam and green banana. When she finished cooking, she portioned food out to everyone; then she'd call me to the back step and hand me my food. I never got into the dining room, much less to the dining table. I simply took what she gave me under the house with the animals.

It didn't take long for name calling to begin. Soon, I wasn't Girly anymore. I was Black Ugly Monkey. My mother forbade me to walk on her floor with my black feet or touch this or that with my black hands. My sitting room was under the house, with chickens, goats, pigs, and dogs sharing the dirt floor. I was guaranteed to be dirty with chickens flapping their wings kicking up dust everywhere. Skin lotion? I never knew what that was; my lotion was sour orange squeezed into last night's urine from the chimmey, which I would mix and let sit for a while, then wash my feet with to prevent them from being ashy and dry. I don't know what happened chemically in that bottle, but it worked because my feet and legs became smooth and the sour orange cut the piss smell.

For a year, these were the things that defined my life. My stepbrother George tried to soften the blow by sneaking me treats when my mother wasn't home. And on Fridays, he made sure I ate well. He could see she didn't treat me well and was upset about the abuse. "You are her only child. Why she do you like that?" I thought to myself that someday I would find out. At times, I also thought about the Jonases—the only parents I'd ever known—and imagined how they must miss me.

I'd left when I was thirteen. I had been ripped out of there. My father, though, passed word to the Jonases when he learned what my mother had done. The Jonases, concerned for my welfare and totally in the dark at first, had instituted a search. They approached my father, and he filled them in. When my father passed by on his way to church, my mother pointed him out to me. My father was a conduit of information to the Jonases. He knew I was there and told the Jonases so they would stop searching and worrying. But nobody ever told me this had happened. I had no clue.

Tears came because I couldn't understand why my mother treated me so badly. It was like she had a grudge against me. She took me from the Jonases. She had me sleep on old rags nobody wanted. My playroom was in the dirt under the house with the animals. Why? What had I done except be me? None of it made any sense. I could not sit on a chair in the house. I was passed meals from the backdoor, accompanied by a glare. I couldn't even go into the house until it was time to go to bed. There was no milk, no touch, no love, just that accusatory eye from the one who'd stolen me from my home. If perchance I didn't hear my mother call me to eat, I missed out. Actually, I'd wind up going into the pigs' food, which I'd prepared myself. It was made up of yams, bananas, cocoa, taro root, dashine, and salt—a gourmet meal for someone who was hungry. The only time I got a smile or a meal made with love was at school because my great-aunt Rachael was head cook and knew about the treatment I endured at home. She'd look for me in the line, make sure I got a nice lunch, and give me hugs and kisses, topping them off with a smile. I think some of the other children were jealous of me because she made such a fuss. They didn't realize this was the only affection I ever received.

Sometimes I'd help my aunt in the school kitchen. It was a chance to demonstrate how much I could do with food and cooking, my passion. I loved it!

Plotting to Leave

When I went home after school, though, I felt like a prison inmate returning to my cell from a work-release program; my steps were heavy with dread about what was coming. I prayed every day for rescue as I walked down the small hill and over the bridge to the house's gateway. I went slowly and counted my steps, trying to take more time. Inside the gate, the yard was paved with cement because my mother didn't like to walk on dirt. I often met her man sitting on a veranda chair. People called him Jakey, short for Jacob. He was laid back and tended to be kind. I'd greet him with a "Good evening, Master Jacob," and he would reply, "How you do?" in Jamaican patois. He rarely spoke to me when my mother was around. I could tell he didn't like how she treated me, but he never said anything, probably because of her temper. I think he also have felt a little guilty about helping to steal me away from the folks who had raised me. After greeting him, I would head to my sitting room and the animals, my best friends.

Even at the age of thirteen, given the conditions I faced, I began to feel a real hatred for my mother. I'd been told she was dead. I'd had no relationship with her; I didn't even know her. Sometimes I'd wish I knew what a mother's love was like, but I never did. And I'd had enough of beatings and eating with the pigs, goats, and chickens. I plotted how to run away, when to run and where. One day I did take off, to my stepfather's brother's home, and my mother had to come fetch me. I was terrified when I thought about what she would do to me because she didn't hesitate to treat me like a criminal, and my punishment was lashes before going to jail. This time was no exception. She hit me with her man's wide black cowhide belt, which left marks on my skin. I ached for days, and that was enough. I decided I'd do anything to get away from her, so I consciously avoided her, quit school, and went to look for work.

I eventually found a job as a maid for a white couple and their baby. They lived in Golden Springs, about an hour away. I was happy to find this family, as I excelled at housework, and it kept me away from my mother. The white family had a six-bedroom house, and my assignment was to cook, clean, wash, and take care of the baby. It was a lot of effort, but I welcomed it, as they paid me ten shillings a week. Since I went to work at such a young age, I lost time in school I couldn't make up. I missed much of the content of classroom subjects and eventually lost interest in school altogether.

The job didn't work out either. It became too hard for me, and I had to quit and go back to the dungeon at my mother's. But I kept contemplating my next move.

By this time, my mother was planning her wedding, the "royal wedding" as the neighbors described it. Of course, you-know-who was *not* asked to be a part of the ceremony; once again, Cinderella was missing the ball. I was now almost sixteen. My peers and sundry nieces and nephews came to be measured for gowns and suits. They shopped for accessories and all the things needed for a wedding, but nothing was done for me. I made the mistake once of asking if I could participate, and the reply was a slap in my face and being told how ugly and black I was. "No, you can't, you little bitch."

As the wedding date drew nearer, I thought more and more about running away. I didn't want to face the shame of being kept in the back of the house, forbidden to show my face to the guests. I simply couldn't deal with it. So four months before the wedding, on a Friday after my mother left for market, I ran away again.

Returning to the Jonases

I went to my father. It was the first time I'd been in his house. We were in the process of getting accustomed to this new arrangement when he told me Grandpa Jonas had died. This made me sad, and I wanted to go back there to pay respects at his funeral. I had no money and had to beg for some to make the trip. It had been two years since I'd seen the Jonas family.

When I arrived, though, the Jonases wouldn't talk to me. It was as if I were a stranger. I really couldn't blame them. Imagine having raised someone else's child between the ages of three months to thirteen years, only to have the mother come back and kidnap her without a word, and then have the child appear again after years had passed. They were very distant as I mourned Grandpa. I tried to explain what had happened to me, but I didn't make much headway, because they thought I'd actually approved of my kidnapping. By nature, Jamaican people are suspicious, and so the Jonases assumed I was in on it.

Also, Rupert, who is now my husband, his grandmother, and my mom were best friends. I didn't know that. The grandmother, named Icy, was a link between my mother and me through the first thirteen years of my life. My mother used to give her things to bring to me: hair ribbons, money (a two-and-sixpence piece), other things. When I went to their shop to buy groceries, Icy would give these things to me, and say, "from your mother." I'd tell her, "I don't have a mother; she died," because that's what my dad had told me. But I took the things anyway. And my mother had known I was at the Jonases all along. So she knew where I went to school because Rupert's mom walked all the kids to school, including me. All this went on around me, but I was oblivious to it.

That's not all. Rupert's grandmother went to the same market we did, so she knew where our stall was, and that I usually helped my grandma on market Fridays. I figured my mother went to the market first, saw I wasn't there, then was told by Rupert's grandmother that I was at school putting on a home economics demonstration. She never admitted she did that, but I think that's what happened and how my mother found me to take me away. The irony is, today I'm married to Icy's grandson.

So there I was, by myself, suffering yet another loss. I went to them with every intention of staying and never returning to my mother, but they would not accept me back into their lives. I tried to understand, but I'd also made up my mind I was not going back to that environment of madness with my mother. After Grandpa's funeral, the Jonases let me stay for two weeks. Then I had to leave.

CHAPTER 9

ON THE ROAD AGAIN

Going to My Father

I WENT BACK TO MY father, although he had no clue I was coming. When I arrived, he was surprised but not so shocked. It was as though he expected me to come to him sooner or later. He knew about the conditions I faced at my mother's house, and I'd talked to him from time to time when he walked by on his way to church. I'd wait to see him every week. I'd wave sometimes, say hello sometimes.

My mother had checked with him, trying to find me, and he'd told her I'd gone to the Jonases.

I was seventeen years old, a vagabond again, and furious with my parents for bringing me into such a brutish world. I wondered what my life would be like going forward. I prayed and asked God to keep me from harm if things did not go well with my father because by then I'd really had it. It was about time for hell to disappear and a little heaven to show itself.

I'd never lived with him before and had no idea what to expect, especially after the experience with my mother. He didn't live alone but shared his small, two-bedroom house with his granddaughter, Alice, a boy he was raising, and his great-granddaughter. His house was situated on top of a hill overlooking the road, where we could watch cars and foot traffic. It was not a bad view, actually, as we could also see houses and the surrounding neighborhood.

My father, a tall, slender, handsome black man, was well respected by young and old. He was educated and well spoken, a mentor who took care of people, a dynamic organist—the first man to play pipe organ in the whole of Saint Andrew Parish—gifted and talented, a former public health inspector, choir director, and voice coach. He was often called on to perform for events.

He tried to teach me to play the organ but was very rough. He'd hit my fingers when I made mistakes. I didn't like that and stopped going around for lessons. But singing was another story; he definitely taught me how to sing. I sang in the choir and solos and accompanied him to functions to sing. I was good at performing because I loved the attention; audiences often said, "Encore, more, more!"

I think he became proud of me; at least that's how it looked. I loved watching his straight, skinny body sway to the organ music on Sundays. I wondered what he was like in his younger days. He never tolerated any of us staying home from church unless we were sick, but he didn't have to worry about me, because I loved going to church.

His parenting, though, was not good, because I was a "bastard child," as others called me. Things were sort of hush-hush where I was concerned. But once I lived with him, that cat came fully out of the bag, so I settled in and worked to know everybody.

Alice showed me who the real boss was: she was. She made it clear she didn't view me as a true relative, and steadily picked at me.

Alice's mother was my only sister; her name was Edna, and she was a tragic figure. She died at a very young age, the victim of a seizure, and I never got to know her. Many times I wondered what our lives would have been like had she been with me as we grew up. It was sad, for both of us.

Compensating for Deficiencies

Before long, my dad introduced me to Saint Theresa Catholic School. I did well there and became friends with the teachers; eventually I was singled out to perform more and more duties. I baked and cooked and basically became the help staff all over again because I was good at it. My teachers approved and told me I would be a good housekeeper, wife, and mother someday. They never caught on that I was compensating, because I had a learning disorder (we didn't know about things like dyslexia then), and worked extra hard at subjects in which I excelled. When I couldn't do the classwork (especially math), I'd ask to work in the kitchen, where I could be productive.

To this day, I read books from the back. I look at the last word on the last page and if it isn't an interesting word, I won't continue. If it is interesting, I'll go to the beginning of the last chapter and read from there. I always want to know the end before the beginning. This is what I have always done; it is my style of reading. In school, they thought I was cheating, but I was just trying to see how the story ended. It took coming to America and working for Kaiser Permanente to learn I was dyslexic. When I would do a patient's chart notes, I would start at the back, and the supervisor would tell me, "No, don't do that." My condition came up when I tested for other positions. I would write as fast as I thought, but when I was done, the words were wrong. When I tried to articulate something, it wouldn't come out right, and when I tried to fix it, it was worse, and I'd look stupid. People didn't say anything, but I could sense what they were thinking. I became terrified about speaking in public. I graduated from high school but don't know how. The only things I liked were home economics and horticulture because they required working with my hands and little else.

I think that's why I liked to see things grow. Plants don't talk back, belittle me, ask questions, or judge. They simply grow or don't. I could tell my plants loved me because whenever I was gone and someone else tended them, they didn't do well. And when I came back, they'd raise their heads in thanks.

My father learned about me at the same time I learned about myself. Some of it wasn't pleasant, because I had developed ways of coping that could have put me in prison. They were how I expressed the deep anger I felt about my life, but soon showed themselves to be a path to destruction instead. I would steal anything that wasn't nailed down, whether I needed it or not. When people found out, they went to my dad. And Alice would bail me out and squash the situation so I wouldn't get in trouble. Once I embezzled money from a lady, and she went to my father. His mindset was to let me go to jail. But Alice knew the people and convinced them I'd pay them back if given a little time. And she helped me pay it back. I was tempted many times to put bad hurt on Alice for acting like she was my mother and constantly breathing down my neck. But thank God she was there because she knew what was going on with me, and when I got in trouble, she came to my rescue.

On Saturdays, Dad would leave the house, and Alice would give me a list of cleaning chores to do while she sat and watched. I rebelled sometimes, and we'd get into fights. Then she'd tell my dad, and I'd get a whipping. I decided right that if I were going to get whippings, it would be for something worthwhile. Once I purposely broke plates because she pushed me so relentlessly and made me mad enough to want to hurt her. Another time, I was in the kitchen making porridge and decided this was the day she would die. I sprayed bug spray all over the kitchen; some got into the porridge, and I did not tell anyone.

My dad came home and went into the kitchen to help himself to some porridge, but he smelled the bug spray and saw the oil residue when he lifted the lid. He asked me about it, and I said I'd been spraying for flies in the kitchen but didn't know the spray had gotten into the pot. He didn't believe me and said he would take me to the police. Then I broke down and told him the truth. He in turn told my mom, and she told everyone else t how I'd almost poisoned him. After that, Alice was afraid of me because she thought I was unstable. She didn't completely stop her pressure tactics, but sensed I could be dangerous so she never came at me hard again. I've always regretted my actions that day, and I've never been proud of that period of my life. Lord, if she'd eaten my porridge and died, I would surely be in prison and never would have lived the life I deserved.

As time went on, my father tried to parent me more closely, but I still wasn't sure about him or much else. On my mom's "royal wedding" day, for instance, he told me he was going and asked if I wanted to come. I told him no. Then I went down the hill, sat by a coconut-tree stump, and watched the procession go by. My heart began to ache. *Why is all this happening to me?* I wondered. *This is my mother. I am her only child, and yet I get treated like trash. How can that be?* A man began bothering me, saying disrespectful things about my dad, and I told him to leave me alone. I hit him and kept on hitting him until I was tired. Then he left me alone, and I went back to the house, without telling a soul what had happened. It was due to shame, anger, and embarrassment that I hit that man.

I was a terror because I was so angry. I took out my frustration and aggression by fighting, and I was a good fighter. I didn't even check to see if the other person still had a pulse when I was done. I fought more men than women because they did things to women without caring, so I had no respect for them.

My father came home from the wedding with all the details about the goings-on (as if I cared). I soon found passersby had informed him about the way I'd hit the man.

The next day, he questioned me about the incident, and I explained why I did what I did. He could see that I was holding much inside. I'd swear at anything and everything. If a fly sat on me, it triggered anger. Ignorant people triggered even more. I had no fear, no self-esteem, no self-control, no shame, and was very negative. I was also very physical. I never lost a fight and didn't care if the adversary were big or small. I never needed urging to fight either, and it was my pleasure to take off my clothes and fight naked because the other guy would *not* have the pleasure of tearing mine off. I set out to demolish anything in my path, including my parents. My only friends were people who behaved like me. I was a gangster, a savage.

In Jamaica, at that time, there was little understanding of mental-health issues like post-traumatic stress disorder. People were "just bad" or "needed a whipping." Even in school, I got into fights. But two teachers—Mrs. Hilton, the principal, and Miss Walters, the vice-principal—felt sorry for me, were compassionate toward me. and wanted to see me get ahead. They understood my situation and helped me along, allowing me not only to learn more in the kitchen but also to become creative in the dishes I prepared. In time, my experiments became lunch delights at school, filling the bellies of all the students. Because of these teachers' efforts, I graduated with my class at the age of seventeen. Neither of my parents attended the ceremony.

CHAPTER 10

GROWING UP

Finding a Place in the Work World

AFTER GRADUATION, I INTERNED AT the post office on Saturdays with Mrs. Rochester, the head postal mistress. She taught me the functions of being a postal clerk and taught me well because eventually I became a paid staff member who worked under her supervision. Later, I secured a position as a postal mistress at another location. With this new position, I was able to pay for transportation to school, so I enrolled in trade school at night. That wasn't bad for a beaten-down bastard child.

But don't think we're done with my mom's story. She and my stepfather hadn't been married long before they had a huge fight, and my mother moved out, never to return. Even though she'd been abusive to me, I felt sorry for her and supported her decision to leave because she'd taken abuse from him too. She went to live with a man she'd met at the market.

While I worked at the post office and attended night school, I still lived with my father, Alice, and her daughter. I studied English, German, and archaeology at the University of West Indies. With my income, I was also able help to remodel the house, purchase furniture, and even buy the first vacuum that place had ever seen. My anger seemed to cool a bit too, with the personal success I was having, and because my heart was warmed by a gentleman named Erick.

Erick

Erick worked for the government as an auditor; he ensured there were no discrepancies, and on my watch, there never were. I did not think about a relationship with him at the time, because I considered government people as police, and in my experience so far, police never meant anything good. Besides, I was nineteen and too young to be tied down, or so I thought.

After Erick finished his work, we would strike up a conversation. He was a serious sort who didn't laugh a lot and was straight-faced. He was more educated than I was, but I enjoyed our talks nonetheless; they were thoughtful and deep. He asked if I had a boyfriend. I told him I had someone but not exactly a boyfriend. I actually had several male friends, but Papa (as I now called him) had higher expectations for his daughter than that lot, and I guess I did too.

Several weeks passed, and Erick asked if he could take me to the movies. I told him that would be nice because I enjoyed his company. After the movies, we talked a while, just casual friends getting to know each other. From then on, we talked every day at work, and on Sundays we went out with friends. Sometimes we'd take long drives in the countryside and find a spot for a picnic. Our friendship gradually developed into a romance. Erick was not only a nice man, but a manly man, older and more experienced with relationships. I was still scared of men because of the experiences I'd had, but Erick seemed to be different.

Back then, every woman wanted a man with a car, and Erick had a car and a house, even though his mother lived with him. Since I still lived at my dad's, we mainly spent time at his house. This didn't please his mother, but it worked out because she and I had opposite schedules. She was a nurse who worked the graveyard shift, and I worked during the day. Erick took her to work at night and stopped along the way to pick me up from the university. I studied German because I worked with a lot of people at the post office who had pen pals in Germany, and I wanted to help them communicate better. I took archaeology because I was fascinated by mysterious things. When something was unearthed, I wanted to know its age, where it came from, and everything. I thought that's what I wanted to do for a career, but Erick told me I'd have to go deep into the bush to do that sort of work and sometimes archaeologists died searching for artifacts. I decided backpacking in the wilderness in search of dead bones was not for me after all.

At Erick's house, we listened to country music, made meals, and hung out together. We avoided intimacy, though. We had desires; we just chose to abstain. In Jamaica, you see, you need your parents' approval to take a relationship to the next level. My dad would have grilled Erick to the point of wanting to know every scar, freckle, and birthmark, and we weren't quite ready for that kind of scrutiny. So when Erick took me home, he only walked me halfway up the hill before he bid me good night.

As our relationship deepened, I was transferred to a military post office in a beautiful town called Newcastle, in the Blue Mountains about two hours away. I regarded Erick as a serious boyfriend, a man with whom I could spend the rest my life. We were very much in love, or so I thought, so he didn't mind driving to the military camp and sneaking into my barracks to stay the weekend. At the camp, unmarried couples were not allowed to have sleepovers. Erick drove a smoky, noisy, gray Volkswagen that announced its coming. I could hear gears crunching when he shifted and knew he was on his way. I was always happy when he was with me.

Another young man took an interest in me around that time. He knew I was dating someone, but pressed me to tell Erick not to come back anymore. I didn't tell him, because I was happy and in love with him and wanted things to remain as they were. Then, during one of Erick's visits, someone slashed all four tires on his car. The next morning, he found his car with the tires flat, immobile. My roommate's boyfriend, who also broke the rules and stayed nights, helped Erick repair his car. But after that, Erick said he wouldn't come to see me under that strict policy again. Faced with that, I spoke with the commanding officer and got permission for overnight visits and clearance for Erick to stay with me whenever he wanted. I also made it clear to the military officials that we were quite serious, and it was hard to be away from him during the week and on most weekends.

Training with Soldiers

Several Jamaica Defense Force soldiers were fond of me and encouraged me to try out for the military. There weren't any women in the military then, but these fellows were willing to entertain the notion on a trial basis. With my high energy, they thought I'd make a good candidate. With another woman, the sergeant's girlfriend, I began to train alongside them.

We trained in the evenings after work. The other woman didn't do so well, but I became one of the boys. I exercised with them, ran obstacle courses, shot at targets with high-powered rifles, and was a fast runner. I did everything they did; I just wasn't listed on their all-male roster. I dedicated myself and learned how to be a solder, to embrace military purpose and discipline. I learned how to defend myself, became more aware of my surroundings, and found I was no longer afraid to look people in the eye.

Becoming Pregnant

For eight months, I went to work in the morning, trained in the evenings, and spent weekends with Erick, either in Newcastle or Kingston. Then I discovered I was pregnant and was asked to quit training. Before the post office found out I was with child, I was transferred to Matilda's Corner, closer to Kingston; Erick was only twenty minutes away. I needed a place to live and had few choices, so I went to Uncle Stanford for assistance. Thankfully, he and his wife, Aunt Clarice, welcomed me into their home. I wasn't a child anymore, and helping me made him feel good about himself.

I wasn't pregnant long before I found out Erick didn't really want kids. He already had one son from another liaison and wasn't interested in having more. It didn't matter to me. I was determined to keep this child, and I told him as much. And I have to say, despite his reluctance, Erick did come to see me while I was pregnant and was romantic and nurturing, feeling my belly with our baby moving around inside.

Erick didn't like Stanford, so he usually visited me during the day while was at work. But the larger I grew, the more distant Erick became. He began spending time with another woman, someone he already knew. She was much younger than I was, a person—as I learned later—he'd been committed to secretly all along. Fact was, that man could have had ten women, and none of us would have known because he was so sneaky. Looking back, I remember his mother saying things to me, snide things she knew

I wouldn't understand because I was sort of naïve and thought he was a straight-up guy. Maybe I was the other woman because his real woman lived next door to him. I never saw her, because he never brought me around when she was at home.

When my pregnancy began to show, I lost my job at the post office. In Jamaica, pregnant single women couldn't work in civil service. I used what little savings I had to care for myself, and Aunt Clarice helped as well.

I had this notion that people changed and mellowed the older they got, so I didn't expect Stanford to behave badly once he was a married man and I was a grown woman and pregnant. Still, I was careful not to be alone with him, just in case he got the urge to strike again with his private parts or try to hit me. He never laid a hand on me, although it was not for lack of trying, but verbally he never missed a beat.

Aunt Clarice was not so lucky. She was an upright Christian woman, but he would beat her and accuse her of terrible things. She begged him for mercy. "Stanford, please don't hit me. I'm not doing anything, I swear. Don't hit me!" When he finished, he usually wanted sex, and if she refused, she was beaten again. Her screams pierced my ears and soul, but I couldn't intervene. I was pregnant and needed to put my baby's safety first. Otherwise, I'd have gone after him, tooth and tong.

I asked Aunt Clarice why she put up with it; her answer was, "Only God knows." There were no laws back then against spousal abuse. As a woman, your duty was to honor, obey, and take what you got, period. I often heard her praying when Stanford was away, asking God when her trial would end and begging for relief from his beatings. But in their house, Stanford was the Almighty because he wrote the Bible on abuse.

In one eerie, predictive conversation, I heard Aunt Clarice tell Uncle Stanford, "Those hands you use to hit me, and those feet you use to kick me—I am the one who'll have to wash them when you are feeble and unable to do even simple tasks for yourself. It will be up to me to take care of you, with the help of God."

And karma later came to his door. Uncle Stanford went into a vegetative state in his early seventies. Aunt Clarice had to wash every part of his body, with help from family members. I only wish Uncle Stanford was more aware during that time and knew the karma wheel had turned, and that the wife he'd abused now controlled his every move. The mighty fell off his throne.

After he died, Aunt Clarice lived in the same house, surrounded by family, until her death. I am happy she enjoyed a few good years without Stanford in her life. After all, God does answer prayers.

CHAPTER 11

I BECOME A MOM

The Birth of My Daughter

WHEN THE TIME CAME TO deliver my baby, Erick was nowhere to be found. It turned out he had left the country. History repeated itself because my own father had disappeared at my birth, leaving my mother to go through labor by herself. I didn't have much, but unlike my mother, I was filled with love for my baby, despite Erick's absence. I also had the love of some family members.

It was a Friday morning. I awoke feeling pain. I dressed and made my way to the doctor's office—it was my checkup day— then stopped at the market on my way back to buy some food. I returned to the house and that evening, I went into labor, and things became a blur. I had to make my way back to the hospital with the help of the Sprouls, two people who loved me and my unborn child. They worked at the hospital. Mr. Sproul drove me to the hospital, and Mrs. Sproul went into the labor and delivery ward with me. While I was in labor, a nurse told me I'd had a phone call from a man named Erick, who said he was sorry but he'd had an emergency and had to leave the country. I couldn't think of an answer to give him, because the pain was too great. All this was passed to me secondhand because I couldn't answer the phone, but I didn't want to talk to him anyway. The labor went on for eight hours; it felt like someone was cutting into my belly and my back at the same time. Then the midwife said "Give one more push" and here came my bundle of joy.

My first child came into the world just before midnight on April 2, 1971. I was sad that Erick kept tabs on me from an airplane leaving the country. It was a great gesture for him to call and offer fatherly support on the day of his daughter's birth, but that was as far as it went. Aside from that phone call, I did not hear from or see him again for a year.

I stayed with Uncle Stanford and Aunt Clarice until my daughter was six months old. Then Stanford asked my dad to come get me. A longtime friend named Dalbert, who drove an ambulance and wanted to date me before I met Erick, moved us and our belongings to my dad's house, but not before my dad gave me a tongue-lashing based on whatever Stanford had told him. To this day, I can't tell you what that was about. I had a bed, suitcases, clothes, and a crib. Although I didn't regard Dalbert in the way he hoped, we remained friends, and he came to my aid more than once.

I didn't want to go back to my dad's, because I knew Alice would be constantly in my face, so I decided to try living with my mom again. This was perhaps an odd decision given what she'd put me through before. But she'd visited me at Uncle Stanford's and never showed resentment, so I thought it would be okay and that things had changed. Anyway, I wanted her to know her first grandchild and be a part of her life. I wanted her to have a chance to be the mom she never was to me.

So my baby and I settled into a room at my mom's place, which was attached to the house but accessed from the outside. It was like a little apartment, only without a kitchen or bathroom. No sooner did we move in, though, than the trouble began again.

Whenever she was angry at me, she'd lock the kitchen door, and I'd have to ask a neighbor to heat water for the baby's milk and a cup of tea for me. Mama also kept me out of the main house. When she went to the market, she never brought us anything—not that I expected her to; it wasn't in her nature. When she cooked, she only occasionally offered food to us. Fortunately, I had a little money of my own, so I bought what we needed. But whatever I had to do, I'd finish it before she came home because I wasn't allowed inside when she was there. I also had friends who knew about the situation and brought food for me and my baby.

I remember one Sunday especially. Mama left for church, so I went to the kitchen to make breakfast. While I was cooking, her man friend came and grabbed me from behind, trying to touch my breast. I had a spoon in a pot on the stove, and I swung around and slapped him in the face with it. Because the spoon was so hot, it took his skin off. He ran away into the bushes. When Mama returned from church, she asked where he was. I didn't answer. It wasn't until nightfall that the man returned. Mama asked, "What happened to your face?" He said he'd been scratched by a bean bush. I wanted to laugh out loud, but I never told her anything, He was kinder to me than she was in many ways; he just couldn't keep his hands to himself.

A year after my daughter was born, Erick came to see me with a gift for her—a dress, one measly dress made in Jamaica. It was a nice dress, but it was nothing. I would have preferred him to bring baby food, or diapers, or toys, or money for necessities, but instead he brought a little white dress she probably wore once. I had not heard a word from him for a whole year, and he just showed up, hoping to rekindle our relationship. Well, despite how angry I was about his neglect, I was lonely, and it was good to see him.

So we became intimate, but it didn't take long before things went sour again and his bad habits raised their ugly head. He started an affair with a young girl who lived right down the street from my father's house. When I found out, I immediately severed our relationship; the pain of the past was too much to relive. Later, I learned the reason Erick disappeared while I was giving birth to his daughter: it was to be with his girlfriend; he was preparing for their wedding.

He eventually married the girl and lived abroad. He didn't maintain a relationship with his daughter for a long time until she moved to live with me in the United States. She tried to have a relationship with him, but it was short lived, and she doesn't have one with him today. When her oldest son, Erick's grandson, was graduating from high school, I made the mistake of calling him with the news, and we got into a heated argument. He told me not to call him again, and I never have. Some people just aren't cut out to be parents.

In retrospect, I have no idea why Mama treated us so badly. Even if I deserved that treatment, my daughter was just an innocent baby. She wouldn't even leave me food to give to her own granddaughter. Mama was just plain evil far as I was concerned. After a few months of living with her, I was ready for whatever I had to endure at my dad's house, so I asked if the baby and I could live with him.

Surprisingly and sadly, I didn't learn much from this experience. I wasn't reflective; my mindset was on the here and now. I didn't look forward or back, just at what was in front of me. It was not so good, but that's the way it was.

CHAPTER 12

THE MONSTER MAN COMETH

George

LIFE IMPROVED WITHOUT ERICK AROUND. I picked up where I left off in school, enrolling in subjects that drew my interest, and I worked at an awning company in Half Way Tree. My baby and I still lived with my father. In the mornings, I usually took the bus to work. A lot of us shared the same stop and waited for the bus together. One man in this group seemed friendly and pleasant, and I looked forward to seeing his face each day. I learned he worked for a welding company run by his family. His name was George; he was eight years my senior, clean-cut, and handsome.

Time passed, and George and I became acquainted. Our first date was on a Wednesday. I remember because on Wednesdays, we stopped work about noon, a common practice among Jewish and Syrian businesses in Jamaica, which is what most of the businesses were. We went to a movie.

Afterward, George took me to Tasty's Patty, a local diner, where we ate and talked before taking the bus home. He always walked me the mile home from the bus stop, but never came up to the house. He'd walk me halfway up the hill, then we'd sit under a big mango tree and talk, then I'd accompany him a ways back down the hill. Up, down, and so on until he was ready to leave.

I'd never dated a man quite like George. His gentleness was endearing to me, and when he spoke, he sounded like someone who wanted a woman to be with and bear his children. I began to envision sharing a stable life with him, but we were both cautious and took our time learning about each other over the course of a year. I thought he respected me, maybe because he knew my father was highly regarded in the community. When we finally decided to take our relationship to the next level, George came to meet my family before I moved in with him in Kingston. My daughter stayed with my father and my sister while we got settled.

At first it was just the two of us, but George had another son from a previous relationship who came to visit occasionally, as did my daughter. The boy usually lived with his mom, but George wanted him with us, so one day while he was with a sitter, he went and took the baby and kept him. The baby's mom was probably afraid of George because she never tried to get him back in the two months we had him.

I had met George's father before, but was in no hurry to meet his stepmother, Din. All I ever heard about Din was she didn't care about anyone except her own children. Soon after we met, Din began trying to control me, going so far as to shadow me when I was grocery shopping, comparing her cart to mine and making assertions like, "The men in this family have a certain way about them." I surmised neither me or my shopping cart measured up to her idea of "their way." It was nice to have a ride to the market, but I chafed under her eye and eventually broke away. I resumed taking the bus.

I liked George's father a lot and called him Daddy. He was a quiet man who wanted people around him to be happy. He was against abuse or insults or unkind words; he was adamant about men beating women, but something behind his eyes hinted at secrets that made him sad and a little fretful. He seemed to want to tell me something, to caution me, but the words never came. I paid little attention to his silent warnings because George and I were in love, and he treated me well—until I became pregnant.

During pregnancy, I wasn't fun to be around. I was hormonal, cranky, sickly, and had no interest in intimacy. George and I began to fight. He called me the nag. It wasn't a pleasant time for either of us. One Saturday afternoon at his folk's house, we were all sitting around talking. His son was resting his head in my lap and, after a while, I needed to use the bathroom. I picked the little boy's head up in my hands so I could slide out from under him, intending to lay him back down gently on the sofa. But the little guy reacted, jerked, and dropped to the floor. He wasn't hurt, just scared. It was an accident.

George, though, thought I'd pushed the boy. So he stood up, picked up his chair, and whacked me over the head. I was eight months pregnant with our son. He knocked me down and opened a two-inch gash in my head that ended up requiring six stitches. Daddy raced to pick me up while George retrieved the boy, and Din yelled, "What are you doing? Don't be killing anyone in my yard." Daddy fetched a wet kitchen towel to cool me down and put pressure on the bleeding, and then Din bandaged my head. My hair, which was very thick and had blocked the blow somewhat, was now clotted with blood. Blood was everywhere. George took the boy and left. I never saw the boy again after that day.

I don't think anyone realized how badly I was hurt, not even me. On my way home, a lady on the bus urged me to go to the public hospital. George and I'd had altercations before, but this was the first time he'd hit me. I was in a daze and couldn't understand why he did it, what I'd done wrong. My head pounded like someone had hammered nails into it. Evil thoughts came into my mind. I wanted to hurt him back, take a frying pan to his head. But now I was aware of his aptitude for rage and understood Daddy's unvoiced concerns. I also had my unborn baby to think about. I wracked my brain, first blaming myself, then trying to figure out what to do so this wouldn't happen again. Three buses and a long walk later, I arrived at the hospital. How I made it without passing out, I don't know. I guess God was watching over me.

The hospital people cleaned my wound, stitched me up, and released me to go home. By the time I'd made it through the front door of our apartment, my anger had turned to shame, then shock, then fear, and I passed out. When I regained consciousness, George was there, standing over me. I struggled to rise, and he helped me to the bed—not gently, but in an assertive, commanding way. A few days later, I found him packing his bag. Here I was nearly at term, wounded at his hand, and he was abandoning me.

Around this time, George developed a fascination with the Muslim community and befriended an older fellow with three wives and lots children. George asked for help with his move, but the old man pleaded on my behalf, saying, "You can't leave her now. Be a man and stay at least until the baby is born." So he did.

My Son's Birth

Though it was two weeks early, I began to suffer what seemed like labor pains. George took me to the hospital, but it was a false alarm and, after examining me closely and asking about the trauma to my head, the doctor sent me home. All I said was,

"I bumped myself." The doctor looked askance at that, but there were no laws about domestic violence in Jamaica then. If there were, I didn't know of them at the time, so away we went.

That night, I went into real labor. My midwife came and helped, but the delivery was long and arduous. I bled a lot, and the midwife worried the baby was distressed, so she called an ambulance. After seventeen hours of painful labor at home, we headed back to the hospital. The medical people immediately identified the problem—my water hadn't broken—so they broke it manually and sent me home to have the baby as planned.

Four hours later, a baby boy arrived. It was a Thursday in February 1974, around 2:00 in the afternoon. He was a big, stocky, healthy boy. And once George saw his son—we didn't know the sex until the baby was born—he decided to remain with me and promised not to hit me again. That was my big mistake.

We moved into a bigger place, renting a room from a man who had a tenement yard. The landlord lived with his girlfriend, Viv. One day, while George was at work, I was cooking porridge on the stove for the baby. When I returned to the kitchen to serve it, I smelled bug spray. I sniffed the baby's porridge, and it reeked of it. I confronted Viv who was the only other person there. She denied everything. I knew she was lying and was very angry, but I kept my cool and decided to let George handle it.

What I didn't know was, from the first time Viv saw George, she'd had her eyes fixed on him. She was jealous of me and made trouble just to get attention, like claiming (falsely) that I'd refused to clean up the kitchen during my turn to cook.

I also didn't know that George had responded to her, and the two of them had become involved. When he arrived home that night, I told him what had happened and what a vindictive witch that girl seemed to be. He told me he'd talk with her, but when he came back, he accused *me* of being the troublemaker! Whoa! I told him I would give her the beating she deserved. George didn't say anything, but instead slammed his fist into my mouth. The ring he wore (which I'd bought for him) split my lip and cracked a tooth. I had to go to the dentist to have my tooth fixed. I thought of leaving, but realized I had nowhere to go.

The next morning while the baby was sleeping and George was at work, I caught Viv rubbing pepper into my underwear. I saw it when I took the clothes off the line. And the lady next door, Mrs. Donnelly, who believed Viv enjoyed hurting people and had no use for her, couldn't wait to tell me how she'd seen the girl do it.

In Jamaica, you could be killed for less, and I wasn't having any more. I grabbed a machete and went after Viv. Just as I was drawing my hand up to slash, George came through the gate and grabbed my arm. While he held me, the girl lunged and hit me, making me even madder. Then she ran while George held me back. I felt confused and betrayed by the man who shared my bed, my life, my child. He was not doing this to save me from spending time in jail, either; he was protecting his whore. I was beside myself. I poked him in the eye with my finger, punching a hole in his cornea. I watched blood and water come out and hoped he would go blind. His scars were nothing compared to mine.

My reaction really surprised and confused him. He didn't know how to regard me. It was apparent I wouldn't take abuse from him. So he didn't say anything; he just went to the hospital to get his eye repaired and came back like nothing had happened. For weeks after that, we didn't talk. His eye healed, but it took a while. And the two of us definitely had relationship mending to do. I had a friend who was a church pastor, and he didn't want us to break up, so we went to counseling with him for about three weeks. We were still living together, but not talking. We decided we had to go slowly. We worked through things gradually and eventually came to an agreement to try again. But we had to move from that house because the girl was a problem. I would have gone after her and hurt her.

We moved into a different place. We did fun things there. We went to the movies, the beach, out to dinner, played games at home, talked and laughed. We were happy and enjoyed each other.

There were occasional signs, though, of George's bad temper. He had a motorcycle, and if he couldn't get it to start, he would lift it and throw it into the gulley. A simple thing like dropping his fork caused him to chuck it into the yard, as if to say, "I don't need you anymore." But I guess I craved love so much, I either didn't see the signs or chose to ignore them. Again.

When we'd go out I had to be careful about how I interacted with people because he was jealous. He didn't even like me talking to my daughter's father. It was odd; when he wasn't angry, he was a sweet person with kind and loving ways, and fun. But whenever he drank, the monster emerged.

Storm Clouds Brewing

A few months passed, and life seemed to be hitting a rhythm in our new home. Things were going better, I thought. Then I became pregnant with another child, and it all changed. George couldn't relate to me when I was pregnant, because I was lethargic and sickly and didn't want to do anything. He was a man who liked sex, and I wasn't interested. He accused me of being with other men, and I told him, "I don't even want you. Why do you think I would want anyone else?"

George started staying out late and coming home drunk. He hit and kicked me. He knew what could happen, that he was putting me and my pregnancy in jeopardy. I don't know for certain, but maybe that was his plan. Then he told me I should have an abortion. I told him I wouldn't do it, that I wanted to have the baby.

But he didn't back off. He pressured me to go with him to a drugstore close to our home where the owner did back-alley abortions. The man looked at me and realized I wasn't a street person or a whore, his usual clientele. I was a beautiful young lady, and he saw in my eyes I didn't want to be there. Since I was already more than thirty days pregnant, he said the only way to abort was to take pills he gave me. "Over time," he said, "you'll feel cramping and eventually just abort." I'll never forget those little brown pills; they looked like chocolate. He give me enough for three days and told us it would take seven to ten days more before I fully aborted and that I might experience bleeding along the way. That was the bottom of the barrel for me as I asked myself, *What kind of animal would place my life and an innocent child's life in danger for his selfish gains?* This was a man to whom I gave myself, even before I was pregnant with either child. I was ashamed. Even now, when I think back, it hurts.

I did feel a little cramping but nothing major, and after three days, I returned to the drugstore alone.

The man asked if he could trust me. "I don't understand," I said. "You're the one dealing with George." The man replied he didn't know George, that he'd come to him via a recommendation from someone else. "I looked at you when you came in," he said, "and knew you weren't like the other girls and street people." He said he could tell I wasn't there by choice, but had been coerced by the man I lived with to do such despicable act. He didn't trust George at all; that's why he didn't give me the real thing to get the job done. I asked, "Are you serious?" The man told me everything he could have done to abort the baby; I would have been messed up badly. I had a guardian angel.

He said the pills he gave me were placebos and wouldn't harm me or the baby. I thanked him for his kindness. "The consequences you'll face when he finds out might be severe, though," he warned, and gave me more of the pills to take home. I didn't care, because the joy I felt knowing that I was keeping my baby made me ready for anything that would come from George. I knew I had help from a higher power. I wasn't afraid of him anymore. I placed the pills where George could see them, and I took them as prescribed. When the pills where gone, he was furious because nothing had happened. He went back to the pharmacist for answers and was told, "Your lady was given as much as she could take without harm, and no more can be prescribed." George came home drunk, angry, and cursing at the man, at me, and at my unborn child. It was obvious he didn't care about us but only his selfish, immature self.

I worked at a factory that made Big Bird costumes and products. On my way home one day, I got off the bus and started walking. I didn't realize George had gotten off another bus and was little way behind me. When he caught up with me, he began to pick a fight with me. When I responded to his babbling, he kicked me down in a gulley; if it had water, I could have drowned. It was filthy in the gulley, full of dog poop, trash, and rocks. I crawled back to the road on my hands and knees and walked home. He walked a few feet in front, smoking a cigarette. At home, I changed out of my soiled clothes, took a bath, washed the stinky, dirty clothes, and prepared dinner like nothing had happened.

After a couple instances of vaginal burning, I made an appointment with an obstetrician. I wanted to ensure my baby was okay. George came with me, not because he cared about me or the child, but because he thought I was screwing around and wanted to see what the doctor would say.

We got off the bus, crossed the street, and made our way to the doctor's office. George started complaining about how we couldn't afford another baby, how he already had two boys and didn't need a third. I said, "Maybe it's God's will for this baby to live because you have done everything you can to stop it, and it's still here. We can split up, and I'll find a way to care for this child." He stood quietly for a moment, lit a cigarette, then whirled around and mashed it into my eye. "I will hurt you badly before you bring another child into the world," he snarled. My eyelashes were singed. If I hadn't blinked when I saw him coming, I would have lost an eye. As it was, I could barely see. Everything happened so fast and I was in such pain, but I kept moving to avoid another attack.

When we arrived at the doctor's office, my eye was deeply bloodshot. I said something had gotten into it. The doctor, not fooled, asked if someone had done this. I said no because there wasn't any benefit in telling the truth; no one cared about my rights. But the doctor knew. "If that cigarette had caught you any closer," he said, "your eye would be gone." He advised me not to rub my eyes, which would make things worse. The eyelash would grow back over time, and the pain would recede.

George was outside in the waiting room. He wanted to talk to the doctor alone, probably about the yeast infection. The doctor said I had a condition common in pregnant women. Always suspicious, George just couldn't believe I wasn't stepping out on him. It was like he needed a way to justify his abuse. And because I wasn't having sex with him, he drew false conclusions.

It took months for my eyelashes to grow back in. I knew what I could and couldn't do, how to avoid the sun and so on, but those were trying days. The doctor told me that the first trimester was the danger period of a pregnancy. I knew I had to do everything possible to keep my baby safe. One day, George met me at the door and tried to kick me in the belly. I turned to the side, and he caught me in the hip instead. It was a hard kick, meant to do damage. I thought my hip might be broken.

Showing no concern, he went downstairs to visit a new girlfriend's apartment. It was clear he no longer cared for me or the baby, so it was time to move on. *Where to?* I asked myself.

I hobbled over to a chair and lowered myself into it. I could hear him downstairs, laughing and talking. I toughed it out because my main goal was to protect my unborn child. I didn't care what he thought; I was determined to have this baby. It was part of me. When George returned the next day, he gathered up his things and some of the furniture and moved into another house with several men and women. God knows what they did there, but I was glad he left.

Of course, I couldn't afford to keep the apartment by myself, so I moved in temporarily with my Grandma Susan, the one who had handed me over to my father when I was a baby. Grandma Susan lived in Mount James, and I stayed with her for two weeks while I looked for a permanent place. Eventually, I found a room for $20 a month at Miss Ruthie, who lived just up the hill.

My oldest son and I lived off savings; we'd never received any support from his father. But money was running out and my little bundle of joy was about to be born, so I went to ask George for some help. When I got to his place, he wasn't around. The landlady said I could wait on the veranda, and wait I did, for about five hours. When he returned, around 10:00 p.m., he came through the gate, smoking, and walked past me without a word. I thought he'd come back out, but he didn't, so I banged on his door. I heard him talking to his friends. One said, "Aren't you going to go out and talk to her?" George replied "F--k that." Several of his friends pleaded with him to come out and talk to me, but he wouldn't budge.

I had nowhere to go. It was too late to catch the bus, and I had no money, so I slept on the veranda on the cold concrete. At times I raised my head when I heard a person's voice, wondering if someone was coming to my rescue. The landlady saw me there in the morning and tried to talk some sense into George. But, as expected, no luck. She brought me a cup of tea and gave me bus money so I could go home. I thanked her and left feeling very sad.

Somehow, I made do without George's help. While I was still working, I had bought baby clothes, and my mother's ex-husband and Alice helped with food and money. Months went by after my last altercation with George, but I had no contact with him. He never tried to find us.

It was hard for me to comprehend all that had happened. Even though I should have drawn lessons from that experience, I didn't do so then. I focused on my coming baby instead.

The Next Son's Arrival

I started having labor pains on a Wednesday evening. I walked up to the road and begged for a ride into Kingston. At the hospital, the nurse told me I wasn't dilated enough and sent me back home to wait some more. Luckily, I ran into my friend Dalbert, who gave me a ride back home. After a very lonely night going through labor pain, I thought, *What if the baby decides to come before daybreak?* I was alone; the hospital was an hour and a half away. *What would I do?* After all that I had gone through to shield this pregnancy, the good Lord kept me and my baby safe. The next morning I really went into labor, and Dalbert took me back to the hospital. My son was born in September 1995. The hospital kept me for two days, and then discharged me and the baby who had fought so hard to make it into the world. Dalbert was my only visitor, and he took us home. I truly appreciated Dalbert.

Six weeks later after I gave birth, George found me. How that happened, I don't know, because I never told him where I lived. I was sitting on my bed with my oldest son, who was playing with his toys, and the new baby, who was about to take a nap. My cousin Fitzroy came to visit me and had also brought me some groceries; he was sitting in a chair by the bed. Without warning, George barreled into the room. I told Fitzroy he was the boy's father, so my cousin thought it would be okay to leave, that I'd be safe.

As soon as my cousin was out of earshot, George started punching me in the face, again and again, until my face was battered and my eyes were swollen shut. My oldest son was frightened and screaming at the top of his lungs, and the newborn was bawling helplessly. When he'd had enough, George left me there, bruised and bloody.

My oldest son stared at me for a long time with fear and tears in his eyes. Then he crawled over and cuddled up to me. I could see how scared he was and tried to comfort him. After all these months of being missing from our lives, George had no right to be angry about anything. All he saw was a man in my room. If he'd bothered to ask, he'd have found out Fitzroy was a relative. I don't think he realized his two children were on the bed with me. He couldn't see past his own rage.

When Miss Ruthie came home, she passed George on his way out. Not knowing who he was, she didn't think much about it. I could hear her in the kitchen, and I called out to her for help. When she saw me, a look of horror spread over her face. She immediately called down to my grandmother's house, and my Aunt Valsie came to see what was wrong. No one had a car, so getting me to medical help was difficult. So they sent for Fitzroy and his wife, Pansy.

Pansy walked me down to her house, put me on her bed, and then went to find someone to take me to the hospital. Even in emergencies like this, I knew favors needed repayment, so I promised money to the man my cousin found to drive me to the hospital. Pansy's sister agreed to watch the kids.

At the hospital, the doctor told me I was lucky no bones were broken. I had soft-tissue damage, but nothing more. He must have worried about a concussion because he told the nurses not to let me sleep that first day so the swelling could abate. With my pummeled face, I looked like a monster, while the real monster ran off without turning around to see if I was alive or dead. Not only did my body ache, my spirit did too. The doctor urged me to file a complaint with the police and obtain a restraining order. A few days later, I went to the Jamaica Constabulary Force in Stony Hill and did just that. They issued a warrant, and George was arrested almost immediately. In court, the judge found him guilty because of the doctor's report and evidence from my landlady. And the court made him shell out money for my medical bills, the only money I'd seen from him in a year and a half. The court also granted a restraining order that required him to stay away from me, and he did because he knew if he came back, my family would kill him. Or I would.

George's father was upset with me because he didn't feel I should have had his son arrested. I believe he knew too well about my problems but struggled with his responsibility and loyalty to his son. For me, a bleak future awaited. Alone and without support, I had three kids to raise and myself to look after. Life would be difficult, I believed.

Relationship Aftermath

As I looked back over the recent chapters of my life, I felt used and cheap. I blamed myself for allowing bad things to happen and wondered if somehow I deserved trouble when it came.

Because I couldn't care for both boys while looking for work, I made the horrific decision to take the oldest boy to George and leave him there permanently. I took my son to his grandparents' house because I knew his father went there every day. I knew if I took the boy up to the door myself, they wouldn't take him from me. So I walked the boy to their gate, opened it, and told him to go on the porch and knock on the door. Then I hid and watched from behind bushes as he climbed the steps. His little hands knocked, making little sound, and I whispered to him, "Shake the door, shake the door."

Eventually George's stepmother came out. She looked at the boy, then checked around to see if I was there. She asked the boy, "Where's your mother?" He didn't know what to say, so he kept silent. I waited, out of sight, until she took him inside. I was hurting so bad because I thought I was giving up my son the same way my mother gave me away. But desperate times called for desperate measures. I was upset and frightened, so I ran. After just a little distance though, I changed my mind and wanted to go back for my son. I was already missing him.

Then I discovered George had taken the boy from the grandparents' home. My job with the Forestry Department had come through; I had an income again and was ready for my son to return to me, but George didn't want to part with him. At one point, he threatened to hire an attorney. George said that since I'd left the boy with his grandparents, I'd effectively abandoned him. I never actually saw George; his father served as intermediary. I told Daddy I would not back down until I had my son. Every day I showed up at Daddy's doorstep, demanding that George bring him back. Finally, Daddy convinced George to give me back my son. At the appointed place and time, my son ran into my arms, and we returned home. Daddy gave me a bag of clothes and food. George sent nothing.

With a job now, I had to find a babysitter for the boys. A friend of Grandma Susan's was willing to help every day from 9:00 a.m. to 5:00 p.m. Her name was Miss Vick, and she was a gift from God. She took great care of my children, and I was grateful.

I didn't see George again until I returned to Jamaica years later to visit my kids, whom I'd left behind in order to set up a better life for us in America. I was on my way back to the United States, and he was working at the airport. The first thing out of his mouth was a request for money. Some very nasty words came out of my mouth in response. I told him if he thought I would give him a red cent after the way he beat me like a dog, he was sadly mistaken. He said he'd been young and stupid and was not thinking. I hurried off before I said anymore because I knew he couldn't hurt me or the boys again.

The second time I saw him was when I was returning to Jamaica. I was taking American wristwatches as gifts, and he asked me for one. I gave him a watch in exchange for his phone number because I wanted my boys to be able to contact and know their father, even though he made no effort to see them while they were still living in Jamaica.

And that wasn't all. As soon as my son was of age, George asked him to file for a green card, so he could come to the United States. And my son did so, and I told Immigration officials that he was a good father, which was a lie. Even though the guy had been awful to us, we found it within ourselves to forgive him enough to make this happen. In retrospect, it was a good thing to do. Today both my boys are grown men with families of their own, and George is a grandfather. And he has a continuing relationship with them.

CHAPTER 13

A FRIEND IN NEED

Policeman Lucas

I WAS A STAFF COOK at the Forestry Service, and we had to walk four or five miles in the dust to get to the forest. Sometimes I hitched rides with the other ladies when their cars had room. Otherwise, we carried big baskets on our heads, filled with supplies for cooking, including water and oil. We had to trek up hills, so we prayed it would not rain. We didn't stay in one location very long, but instead moved from site to site until that project was finished, and we were told we weren't needed anymore.

When the forestry job ended, I became involved with a man I'd known for a long time but never mingled with because George had a stamp on me, warning potential suitors I was taken. Frankly, I could have done without that sort of taking, but every experience in life makes you stronger, and having my two boys and my daughter left me with no regrets.

I had first met this man—his name was Lucas—while working for the post office years before. The police station was right across the street, and I became acquainted with many of the officers. And after the issuance of the restraining order on George, they looked out for me like protective older brothers.

One day I heard a knock on my door.

"Who is it?" I called.

"Police," came the reply.

"You have the wrong house," I said.

"No," he said. "This is the right one, where they told me you lived."

We went back and forth like that for a while, and then he said, "Are you going to open the door, or am I going to have to kick it down?" I was shocked and silent, as you can imagine.

"Aren't you Deloris Barclay?" he asked. I told him I was, and he demanded, "Then open the damn door." I did so and saw Lucas and another officer standing there.

I shouted, "It's you! How did you find me?" Lucas claimed he was patrolling the area. I said, "This is not your beat. You'd have to be looking for someone in particular to be here." He admitted he just wanted to see where I lived, and we laughed out loud.

It made me think. With all I'd been through in life—the places I'd lived, imploding relationships, physical assaults, uncertain support, and dehumanizing situations—I still believed having my children to love and to love me back was worth the pain. But being mother and father to my two boys and my daughter wasn't easy, and I appreciated the fact Lucas wanted to take care of us, bring us food, and other necessities when I wasn't working, to offer us a sense of protection.

At this time, my daughter was three years old and living with my father and my niece, who had been clear about not wanting her to move around with me. My father believed my life wasn't the best environment for a little girl; though he never paid me much mind growing up, he took a more paternal role with his granddaughter. That was okay with me. I got to see her whenever

I wanted and knew she was getting the proper care she needed. My oldest son was eighteen months old, my second son was six months old, and they both lived with me.

I started dating Lucas. He seemed to see me as I was, love my children, and never look for anything other than mutual affection. He did drop in at all hours of the night, though. I never knew when he was coming. There was no warning; he just showed up. I was still reeling from the monster and was not looking for a relationship. We became friends first, but as time passed we became intimate, and I became pregnant with my daughter, child number four.

I let my guard down because Lucas was generous and thoughtful—perfect for me at the time. He was there when I needed him, but I had my own space and freedom too. Everything was going fine until I received a letter from his wife. I had not known he was married, and especially not that the wife had found out I was dating her husband, was pregnant with his child, or even where I lived and who I was. But word got around.

When I received her letter in the mail, my whole body tensed in shock, and my heart sank in confusion, sorrow, and rage. I'd known Lucas forever, and he neither told me he was married nor wore a wedding ring. In retrospect, maybe I should have seen his spontaneous late-night arrivals as warning signs, but he was a cop and that was the nature of the job. I did not suspect him, and I was not the kind of woman to willfully take what wasn't mine.

In the country, all anyone needed was your first and last name, and he or she could send you a letter. The woman in this letter stated that she was Lucas's wife and was coming to claim everything he had ever given me, which would have been food and affection. The question was what would I give back to her because she was not getting my baby.

When I confronted Lucas about the letter, he admitted he should have told me he was married and assured me his wife wouldn't bother me. I didn't believe him, because if I had been in her shoes, I would have been on the warpath myself.

I told Lucas I planned to meet with her because I didn't want any problems, and I owed her an apology. Despite our indiscretions, the baby should not suffer. The baby was coming, and Lucas would need to help care for it, so the best thing was for me to face this situation before it got out of hand. Besides, my self-esteem was at an all-time low, and I needed something positive to happen. Here I was—used again! Had a man, but didn't have a man because he was somebody else's man. Damn!

Meeting Lucas's Wife

I found out Lucas's wife worked at a bookstore store in Kingston, so I went to find her. When I approached her at her place of business and asked to speak with her, she asked if we'd met before. I told her, "I'm Deloris, the one to whom you sent the letter," and showed it to her. Her eyes began to move from side to side, as if her mind was searching for its next move. She was stunned into silence.

Then we talked. I said, "I'll be the first to admit how sorry I was when I found out Lucas was married." I told her I'd never set out to hurt her or anyone and that she was welcome to take anything she thought might belong to her husband because the only thing I had from Lucas was in my belly. "But I'm telling you, I won't give you my baby," I said. I assured her I wouldn't continue an intimate relationship with him, but he would have to help care for the child. I urged her, since she was a mother herself, to encourage him to honor his responsibility. Then she told me

Lucas had other children, not just hers and mine. Lord! We parted on amicable terms, and she wrote to me occasionally to see how the baby was. But I never told her anything or let her see my baby.

The next time Lucas came to the house, he said, "I understand you met my wife." When I asked why he didn't tell me he was married, he said, "You didn't ask." I gave him a look that could push him through walls, and he said, "I thought you knew." I admonished him roundly and loudly for not being honest with me. He told me lots of girls liked married men, and I responded, "I'm not one of them."

Finally, we decided to remain friends because we had been friends before. And today, we still are. He lives in Jamaica. My husband, my children, and I live in the United States. Anytime we go back to Jamaica, Lucas picks us up at the airport. He and our daughter have had some contact through the years, but Jamaican men are very different when it comes to parenting. They believe their job is to go out and work and provide, but they are not as hands-on with children. I think over the years that has changed, but back then, it wasn't a priority.

Giving Birth Alone

My baby would be born at home with a midwife's help, so when it was clear it was my time, my aunt went to get the midwife. But the baby didn't want wait. I was home alone with my two boys, facing the delivery alone. I was concerned, certainly, but not overwrought. I began to prepare for her arrival. There are steps to take to prepare for home births; the first thing to do is put water on to boil. I wasn't sure what I was supposed to do with the water, but I put some on the heat anyway. Then I packed newspaper on the bed, put plastic and disposable sheets on top.

I fed the boys and put them in the crib with some toys. Then, I went to the bed to await my baby. I felt a nagging pressure, as if I had to go to the bathroom, but I knew better. I got one leg out of my panties and positioned myself on the bed, and there came my beautiful baby girl. I prayed, "God, I don't know what to do here. You have to help me with this one." I was lying on my back. I moved my leg out of the way so I could pull her out of me and lay her beside me. I wrapped her in the sheet and anxiously waited for her to cry. She didn't. The cord was wrapped around her neck. I hurried to uncoil the cord so she could breathe. Finally, she began to wail, and I knew she was all right. But I still wondered, *Did I do something wrong? What if the baby is not okay?*

The wait for the midwife was the longest fifteen minutes I've ever spent. I had just pushed my daughter out and now had to do everything necessary to keep her alive. I lay there by myself, thinking that I would rather die than have another child like this. But then I looked at my baby, and she was so beautiful, I knew she was a blessing. I pulled myself together because my two boys were sitting right there, looking at me and probably wondering what was going on. When I first looked at this beautiful little person, I saw she had absolutely no hair on her head. My beautiful bald-headed baby girl! I chose the name Melissa because I wanted my little angel to have a name that reflected her beauty.

When the midwife finally showed up, she was stunned to see that Melissa had already been born. She commended me on the job I did delivering her by myself and said I'd done everything I could have done up to that point. She made me feel better. I didn't have those kinds of skills, so I was scared as hell. The midwife cut the cord and gave me a shot so the placenta would come out. Then, she cleaned both me and my baby and put her in a little nightgown I'd made with my own two hands.

Lucas got word I wasn't feeling well and knew I was in labor. He arrived just as the midwife left. It was September 1976, and he stayed with me the whole weekend, making sure things went well. He also apologized for not telling me the truth about his marital status. He made no excuses. Despite how I'd been brought up, I wasn't a woman who wanted another woman's man. After that, Lucas dropped by once in a while to see how I was doing with the two boys and baby Melissa, but only to ensure we had what we needed.

When Melissa was three months old, I was informed I had to relocate because the family who owned the house wanted to move back. I decided to return to my roots in Halls Delight, where the Jonases had lived, and that's where my life took another major turn.

CHAPTER 14

LIFE GETS BETTER

The Warmth of Rupert Dallas

IN APRIL 1977, WITH NOWHERE else to go, I moved back to the Jonases' house in Halls Delight, where I'd grown up. Grandma and Grandpa had long since passed. Odd son Jonas, now with an amputated leg caused by diabetes, lived in the front of the house. He was still a free spirit who kept to himself and didn't need help. He got around on his hands and knees, crawling for miles, like he had two feet. We'd see him places and wonder how he got there.

I'd come full circle back to my roots, and it was not a comfortable place to be. I didn't want to go to my father's house, because of my niece, who constantly rubbed things in my face. She'd talk about how I shouldn't have done this or that, and how I messed up my life. Her constant badgering could have pushed me to unthinkable actions; after all, I had tried to put a hurting on her once. In Halls Delight, I might get some peace because there were no men left in the district who wanted me, and I surely wanted nothing to do with them!

The back part of the house where I would stay was in shambles from years of neglect. I didn't care, because it was available for me when I needed it most. I wasn't surprised to find I wasn't welcomed warmly by Aunt Icy or her children, who lived down the yard within calling distance. I had my bed and the kids' bed and kept out of sight. I had the basics I needed to keep going and that was all that mattered. I planned to find a way to refurbish the house, so it would be a fit home for my children and me, although with no job and little money, I didn't see how. I just hoped.

Aunt Icy was dating a man named Ossie, who had known me since I was small child. Our community was small, and everybody knew everybody. Another man, Teddy Dallas, lived a mile up the road. In the old days, he raised sheep and would let them out to graze. Any that wandered into our yard, Grandpa shot dead. Teddy harbored no resentment because he knew where Grandpa stood: put away your livestock, or take what you get. People didn't mess with Grandpa. He was mean, ruthless, and knew how to use a gun.

Teddy's wife was named Monica, the big sister of the neighborhood. She volunteered to walk all the neighborhood kids to school, including me. To this day, people still love and respect Miss Monica.

The day I met Teddy's son Rupert, he was with his Uncle Ossie, Icy's friend. It was strange; I'd not known about him before, since his parents were longtime acquaintances of mine, and Rupert lived with them up the road.

Ossie must have told Rupert my house needed repairs because before long Rupert paid a visit to assess my needs. He was president of a local service club and told some of its male members he wanted to help a single mother make her house livable. Spending their own money on supplies, Rupert and three other men begin cutting down trees to help me build a decent house.

I was amazed. *Why was this man being so nice to me? What had I done to deserve this help?* I wondered what he wanted in return. I had no money, no job, and a broken-down home, housing three of my four children from three different fathers. I didn't think much of myself.

Rupert said, "Never mind." He would tell me how beautiful I was, compliment my eyes, my face, my smile. But my self-esteem was shot, and I couldn't escape the feeling of shame that lived in my head. There was something awfully wrong with the way my life had gone so far. I didn't know how to reverse the damage, and I did not want to repeat it. I had my children to consider.

The rebuild of the house happened quickly. The first day, while I was out job-hunting, Rupert and his buddies tore down my side of the house, the very room where Granny and Grandpa had slept, where Grandpa tried to rape me. It was a little like revisiting a tragedy, but I knew Grandpa couldn't hurt me anymore, so I embraced the change. When I came home, Rupert and company were well on their way to transforming that old place into a home we could live in free of worry. In only three days, my house was done.

Before Rupert ever drove a nail, though, he fell in love with my kids. The day we met, I was holding my seven-month-old, Melissa. He took the baby from my arms and held her and played with her. He made funny faces and sounds, and Melissa just loved it, smiling and laughing like a child at her first circus. My two sons, stared in wonder and it didn't take long for Rupert to win their hearts as well. But to win mine, he had much more work to do.

I was in a sad state. I was afraid to date men. My past had eroded my confidence, and I no longer trusted my own judgment. Rupert saw past these fears, was supportive, and we formed a friendship. He came to my house often, and we had long talks. He brought food and treats for the kids and me. I was delighted to discover he liked to cook, and we shared kitchen work and meals. He could take the simplest ingredients and make them taste good. He was a presence, showed interest, and did the right things. Sometimes I'd catch him staring at me, and I ignored him, not wanting to lead him on. I was broken, and that condition wouldn't going to change easily. I never told Rupert about my past. I was too embarrassed and couldn't bear to have him look at me with disgust or disappointment.

It was difficult for me to watch Rupert with my kids because it sort of felt unfair to let him do so much. But I couldn't deny the children this gift of nurture. When AI suffered a nearly fatal asthmatic attack, Rupert carried him on his back for more than three miles to the doctor. He was always eager and available to help, but more than that, he genuinely cared.

In early 1978, I was hired to work at a handbag factory. By that time, I'd been back in Halls Delight for ten months. Every morning before work, I walked a half-mile to the babysitter's house, where Rupert would meet me. From there, we'd walk another two miles to the bus for our morning commute. In the evenings, we'd meet in the square before catching the bus. On days I didn't show to meet him, Rupert would assume I was working late and would retrieve the kids from the babysitter, bathe them, feed them, and put them to bed. And if I still wasn't home before dark, he'd come to meet me along the road because he knew I'd be afraid. The roads had no lights, and the only way to see was to carry a kerosene bottle with a cloth wick.

Deciding to Open My Heart Again

Gradually, I came to trust Rupert and believe he was different from other men I'd known. When he came out late at night to meet me and ensure my safety, I warmed to him. After spending long days sitting at a machine sewing handbags, finding Rupert's dinner waiting on the table at home meant a lot. My heart began to open, and I felt I could love again.

In retrospect, Rupert was the beginning of my real life. We simply connected, I knew at some point soon our mutual interest would become more serious and I'd wind up pregnant again, so I went to a clinic to obtain birth control.

Sure enough, before long, Rupert asked me if we could be more than just friends. This sounded wonderful to me, but first I wanted to tell him about my past. I opened up and told him my life story. Again, he said, "Never mind. All that matters is our relationship. It's a waste of time to worry about what other people think."

I was surprised he wasn't shocked or mortified. He just loved me for me.

"If one man doesn't work out," he said, "you find another." He held nothing against me, and even told me about his cousin who had children from six men and had never been married.

"It's only about you and me," he said. "I'll never bring up your past or talk about it with anyone."

Love and gratitude burst from every vein, pore, and bone in my body. However, in Jamaica, people don't talk about their problems, so I didn't tell him about the abuse.

During a water shortage, when we had to travel some distance with buckets to fetch our daily supply, I realized I wanted to spend my life with Rupert. He emanated pure goodness, and I was hard-pressed to keep denying him. Balancing our pails of water on the trek back home, we stopped in a tamarind grove to rest. I was standing on an embankment when he came down the hill and planted a gigantic kiss on my lips! By no means was I a novice at kissing, but this was different. It was not a kiss I would write home about or one that marked him as a particularly good kisser, but it did tell me he loved me.

We picked up our buckets and continued our journey, not speaking for the rest of the night. The next morning on our way to work, I asked him how his mom and dad would feel about a woman with four kids. He said if they didn't approve, he'd simply move in with me. *No way*, I thought. *I don't want to be another common-law wife.* So even though we seemed to be a real couple, I kept him at bay.

During the week, Rupert worked as an appliance technician. On weekends, he helped in his grandfather's shop, where he gathered groceries for me. Aunt Icy didn't approve of us as a couple and was suspicious about why Rupert treated me so well. To find out, she went to his uncle, who told her how excited Rupert was to date me. Later, I found out Rupert had asked his uncle to introduce us.

Another Child on the Way

I lived in that house in Halls Delight through 1978 and, during that time I became pregnant with Rupert's child. The thing was, I'd never missed taking my birth control, so I couldn't believe how this could have happened. Since the pills eliminated my monthly cycle, I did not suspect I was pregnant until my clothes got tight. I thought I was getting fat. But a blood test confirmed the pregnancy, and the doctor told me to stop the birth control immediately. "Now we just have to find out how far along you are," he said. The answer shocked everyone, especially me. I was three months pregnant!

I started having sleepless nights and restless days, agonizing over the way my life was playing out—pregnant again with a fourth father. And I'd taken precautions. I'd done all the right things this time. Then, morning sickness settled in. On top of that, coworkers encouraged me to abort. As before, though, I refused to do that.

Around this time, Aunt Icy Jonas became even more jealous of my relationship with Rupert and started to harass me. She took my things when I left them outside. She threw dirty, stinky water at my door. My guess was, once the house was renovated, she wanted it. I tried talking to Uncle Stanford, but he didn't believe me. Finally, when I could no longer stand Icy's antics, Rupert suggested I move into his room up the road with his parents. I took my bed, the bed the boys shared, and Melissa's crib for when the baby came, and a dresser. We paid our share of the rent to Rupert's parents.

Rupert and I talked about getting married, but we weren't convinced it was the best option for us. His parents had never married and were still together. The married ones seemed to be the wife-beating cheats. My mother married one man, moved in with another, divorced the first, married the second, then divorced again, And look at the way my papa carried on. Where was the example? I was confused and distraught, but through it all, Rupert sought to make me happy with the little he had.

In the growing season, Rupert planted yams, corn, and peas, which I harvested and sold at the same market I'd gone to with Granny years before. When that was done, I took fresh fish door to door to help us get by.

Meeting My British Brother, Sam

On one of our visits to see Papa, he said my brother Sam, whom I'd never met, was coming from his home in England to visit. He was twenty years my senior, very short and muscular like a bodybuilder, and had big ears. He turned out to be the sweetest man anyone could have for an older brother.

When Sam arrived, he came to see me at Rupert's. He showed affection, never judged me, and talked to me like a father would to a daughter. He never discussed anything negative about my past or resent me for being his father's bastard child. He was genuinely interested in my children and me. And I appreciated that.

Sam's wife had died at an early age, and he'd raised three children by himself in England. My brother was my kindred spirit. He showed true brotherly concern, and we spent much quality time together during his three-week visit. On his last day, he handed me a bundle of English pound notes and said, "I don't know what to do for you, but here is some money." He told me not to hesitate to write him about anything. He also encouraged me to marry Rupert and build a life with him. Not long after he left, Junior was born in January 1979.

Every year after that, Sam visited Jamaica and made a point of seeing me. He'd find me wherever I was, give me a little money, and spend time with my children, who grew to love him. Sam was the only one of my four brothers who ever gave me anything tangible. Even today—he is over eighty now—he asks if I need anything. My two youngest boys like to visit him in England. We reminisce occasionally about our adventures. I hope he lives a long time, because I enjoy him.

Discovering an Age Gap

When we registered Junior for a birth certificate, the application called for his parents' ages. I could see Rupert writing sort of secretively on it. I was still in the hospital recuperating from the birth, so Rupert took the paperwork home. When he returned to pick me up a couple of days later, I asked him, "How old are you?"

He said, "Does it really matter?" I guess my expression told Rupert I wanted the truth because he suddenly confessed, stating, "I just celebrated my twentieth birthday."

Oh Lord, I thought to myself. What will people say about me now? He was just a teenager when we met! I was born in 1949; Rupert was born in '58. I was nine years older. That would not be so bad later in life, but at that age—scandalous. It had never occurred to me that Rupert could be that young, because he was so responsible and much more mature than any of my other children's fathers, who were highly educated. Some worked for the government; another had a degree in criminology. Yet Rupert was more of a man than any of them would ever be, and that was enough for me. Our age difference didn't bother Rupert at all, but it bothered his mother and other family members. They even tried telling him Junior wasn't his baby, but they never would have said that if they'd seen him.

When Junior was born, the nurse looked at him and looked at Rupert and said, "Nobody in the world can tell you that this isn't your child. You guys will look like brothers." His family didn't know this, because they never saw the baby until his first birthday party. At that time, the relatives took one look and couldn't believe their eyes. How could a child look so much like a parent? Siblings yes, but parents? That was why I named him Junior.

When Junior was two, he fell and cut his lip in the same place where George had given me a permanent scar. He was always wandering off to the bush to pick up the fallen fruit. He must have fallen and struck his mouth on a rock. I told Rupert people would think the identical scars were birthmarks, only mine was no accident. That's when I opened up to Rupert about my painful past and the pattern of abuse I'd faced. It made a mournful tale, but Rupert listened to it all.

CHAPTER 15

LEAVING JAMAICA BEHIND

Getting Past Immigration

IN EARLY 1980, WHEN MY youngest son Junior was just a year old, I left Jamaica and traveled to Toronto. In those days, it wasn't necessary to get a visa for Canada, but I did have to have a sponsor and invitation letter. Then, the deal was if I qualified during an interview conducted by Canadian Immigration officials, they'd let me in. Actually, the Immigration people wanted to know if my sponsor could provide for me during my visit, since I wasn't allowed to work.

We were allowed to have only a little money when we arrived. My sponsor, Mr. Newland, met all the qualifications, except one: he was a friend, not a family member. My sponsor was interviewed in a different room, neither of know what the other was saying. It was very nerve-wracking for me; I wasn't used to this.

Finally, after about fifteen minutes, we were all allowed to gather together. My heart was thumping in my chest because I was afraid; I didn't know what to say. I sat straight across from my sponsor, trying to figure out what was going on, when all of a sudden the officer turned his head and asked, "How are you related again?"

I thought it was a trick. I looked him in the eye and said, "I never told you we were relatives. We're family friends."

And Mr. Newland backed me up, saying, "I already told you that." Then he went into an involved explanation of why he'd asked me to come visit him.

To make matters worse, when I looked around, I noticed almost everybody on that flight was being denied and sent back to Jamaica. I was the last person left and terrified. I began to pray. The officer rose from his desk, gathered my passport and the invitation letter, and walked away, saying he'd be right back. I looked at my sponsor with wide eyes. I was thinking maybe I should give up like the rest, but then told myself, *Stop that. You can win out over adversity.*

In a little while, the officer returned with a crumpled piece of paper, which he tossed in the trash. No! With my head bowed and my eyes downcast, I beseeched him in my mind to let me stay, if not for me then for the children! He held my passport in his hand, picked up his pen, and said, "How long do you want to stay?"

Incredulous, I said, "Three months, if I can."

"How about six?" he asked.

Oh my God! I felt like the weight of the ages had lifted from my head. I thanked the man and said "God bless you," probably too many times, and then we left to pick up my bag at the customs counter.

As we walked out to the car, I looked up at the sky and a huge drop of water hit my forehead. I had never seen raindrops that big. It was cold too, like ice.

I asked, "Is that what rain is like in Canada?"

My sponsor looked at me quizzically and replied, "What are you talking about? It's not raining."

It must have been my imagination, or a sign.

We got into the car and drove away. When we were underway, I gazed through the windows at the lights of the city. It was about 10:30 at night; the lights were so bright, and they were everywhere. I decided right then this trip would be an adventure for me. I'd never before been away from Saint Andrew Parish, much less flown to a foreign country.

I told myself, *When I go back to Jamaica, it'll be to bring my children out.* I had left all five behind, a very difficult thing to do. Four were safe and being cared for by Rupert and his family, my eldest daughter still lived with my father, but they weren't with me, which hurt. *I have no time to waste*, I thought, *because I already miss them, especially the baby.* My plan was to do everything I could to keep them from having a childhood like the one I'd had.

The car slowed and stopped, and I looked around for the house where I'd be staying. There was no house. "Get in the elevator and go up to the fourteenth floor," my sponsor said. I did, and voila, there was an apartment—the Newlands' home. It was beautiful and well furnished, but not where I'd have chosen to live because I didn't like big buildings. After about a week, though, I got the hang of things and began to enjoy the place.

A Trip to Michigan

My grand plan, once I was safely in Canada, was to make my way to California somehow to visit my mother and some other relatives. Mr. Newland knew this and arranged for someone to help me across the border. He had a contact in Michigan, the closest crossing point. Because I knew nothing about the geography or driving, my sponsor decided he would have to arrange to get me there. I knew nothing about the people along the route, but there was no turning back.

Good thing, I was prepared to be flexible because we found out two Africans had been assigned by Mr Newland to accompany me to Michigan. And we weren't driving the first leg; the Africans and I were taking a train from Toronto to Michigan. One of the Africans, the smaller one, spoke English well. The larger one didn't. I had a nagging feeling something wasn't right, but I was a stranger in a foreign land and needed to play it out. A lot of thoughts ran through my mind, but I didn't say anything.

The train finally stopped, but I didn't know where I was. The two Africans were in the car with me. They knew who I was from the paperwork my Toronto sponsor had given them, along with a fee for accompanying me. Their job was to get me to the border, then turn me over to other people who'd be responsible for me from there. They took me off the train.

What have I gotten myself into? I wondered. The Africans were conducting their own conversation, leaving me out. I couldn't understand what they were saying. They escorted me to a waiting car, driven by a lady with two babies. I stopped them and told them I was uncomfortable because I didn't know any of them, and preferred not to go to Michigan with them. I was scared.

The two men called Mr. Newland, and he told me to go ahead, that everything was all right. So I calmed down and we got into the car for the trip to the border.

In a little while, we arrived crossed into Michigan. We drove about thirty minutes more—it was 10:00 or 11:00 at night—and arrived at a big white house. When we knocked on the door, a woman, another complete stranger, opened it and said, "Come in." I asked her where Mr. Newland's friends were, the ones I was supposed to meet. She told me they'd arrive in the morning, showed me to a bedroom, and said, "You must be tired after the travel and stress. Get some sleep."

I asked if I could have a drink of water first. She said, "Fine," and took me into the kitchen. Surreptitiously, I scanned the space and spied a big butcher knife on the cutting block. Without anyone noticing, I took it and slipped it into my bag, so I'd have a weapon if things turned ugly.

By this time, my fear had transformed into something more like anger. *What were these people doing? Was I being kidnapped? Was this house like a jail, where I was being kept against my will?* The two Africans had a heated exchange about me and about money. The little guy told the big one, "You got paid. Leave her alone."

In my room, I could still hear the Africans arguing. I kept my traveling clothes on and the knife at hand, just in case. I heard footsteps drumming up and down the hallway. I was spooked and wanted to be ready for anything.

About an hour later, I heard knocking on the door. It was the big African, telling me to open the door so he could talk to me.

I said, "I can hear you. Talk to me through the door."

He got angry and yelled, "I said open the door!" in a deep voice. And he shook it.

But I had wedged a chair under the door handle, and he couldn't push it open. I kept quiet after that. He said foul things in his language, and then the little guy got in his face saying, "Leave her alone, man." I think the big one wanted to rape me. I waited until he was gone before I moved even a little.

It was about 2:00 a.m. by that time. I sat on the small bed and cried. I'd given them my passport earlier for the border crossing and did not know where it was or how I'd get it back. I wondered if this would be the end of my life, if these people would kill me, and no one would ever know or find my body. Since it was now quiet outside my room, I took the chance of removing the chair and tiptoeing out to the railing, where I could see down to the front door. I noticed some papers on a table by the door. *Just maybe*, I thought, *those are my passport, travel papers, and airplane ticket.* I returned to the room and put the chair back. My thoughts got wilder, a situation which was not helped by the fact my room was windowless. I sat on the bed, wide awake, and waited.

My bag was packed, I was still in my travel clothes, and I had the knife. When I heard no sounds and the house lights were all off, I carefully moved the chair away from the door again, took my shoes off, and crept barefoot down the stairs, holding my breath. I snatched all the papers off that table, scooted to the door, opened it (setting off the burglar alarm), stepped into my shoes, and ran. People woke up, but by that time I was off down the street in blind fright. It was about 4:00 in the morning when I ducked into a liquor store not far from the house.

I asked the people in the store where the nearest airport was. They told me I needed a cab because it was too far to walk and dangerous. My heart was beating so fast I could hardly speak. So they called a cab for me. I jumped in, and we tore off. Once at the airport, I hid the butcher knife in the back seat of the cab, got out, went inside the terminal, and started going through the papers I'd taken from the house. Wonder of wonders, there were my passport, airfare, everything—plus paperwork detailing the Africans' arrangement! Thank you, Jesus! I asked a few questions, found my way to the correct airline counter, and checked in for my flight.

Then I looked back and noticed the two Africans coming through the terminal door. But I knew they couldn't say anything about me to anybody. I had the goods on them, and they would go to jail if they did. I turned to them, caught their eyes, and quietly mouthed, "Just try something." Then I turned and walked away. They weren't happy at all.

My plane didn't leave for California until 10:00 a.m., hours later, but I didn't care. I sat there waiting, knowing those guys couldn't get at me anymore. I'd made it out of their trap. I was safe.

CHAPTER 16

ON TO LOS ANGELES

Seeing My Mother Again

CONFUSED AND TERRIFIED ABOUT WHAT had almost happened to me in Michigan, and no longer trusting anybody, I headed directly to Los Angeles, my mother, and my family. I had a six-month visa for Canada and knew I couldn't stay in the United States. I would have to return to Toronto at some point. So while the airplane was crossing the country, I had a lot to think about. I hoped my family could give me some advice.

I landed in Los Angeles around 3:00 in the afternoon. As I left the plane, I looked around at another totally new place, and wondered fearfully what was in store for me now. At the terminal gate, though, I recognized my Aunt Esmie, my mother, and my uncle.

It felt odd to rely on my mother, since we'd never had a good relationship. But, oh well. I told her about my experiences in Toronto and at the border crossing into Michigan, and how scared I was as a result. She assured me everything was okay now, and nothing would happen to me there.

Concerned about my immigration status, my uncle consulted his attorney for legal advice and was told I must return to Jamaica but not before my visa ran out. All right! A door was open, and I had a little time to think about my next steps. I didn't have to go home to Jamaica right away, which was good, because I knew I'd have a hard time getting back to the United States.

I stayed with my uncle and his family for a while; then it was decided I'd be better off with my mother. As it turned out, that was a mistake, as it always had been because her abuse started up again. This time, though, I had no money and no job, so I had to stay and put up with it. She took away my passport and hid it. She also called Rupert in Jamaica and asked him to tell me my son had broken his back; if true, that would have put me on the next plane home. But Rupert didn't play. He called me and told me what she'd said was a lie. My mom didn't know what to do after that, so she returned to her old abusive ways.

More Immigration Hassles

I needed to find a way to get out from under my mom's eye, so I could figure out how to retrieve my children.

My aunt found a job for me, as a nurse's helper at a hospital. There, I met a nurse who had a son named Phill. I talked to her about my children in Jamaica and how I hoped to bring them to America. I shared my angst about this process, and she suggested I speak to her son. I did, and he said maybe he could help me bring them to the United States. I was so thankful.

Phill and I spent a lot of time together after that; we developed a relationship and were married in Los Angeles in January 1981. Shortly after that he filed my immigration papers. The problem was, Phill had some run-ins with the law, so his past wasn't right with the authorities. While we waited for official gears to grind, he got into more trouble. I hired an attorney to help me in case Phill's police record became an obstacle. The day I took my papers up in the elevator to the attorney's office, Phill was coming down. He'd spoken to the lawyer early and signed the necessary documents and so forth because he knew he was going to be arrested. He kept his promise to help me with the children. And he was the first man in my life who ever offered help without seeking anything in return or subjecting me to abuse. When I received my green card six months later, I felt I owed it to Phill. And when my children finally joined me in this country, I took them to see him. He helped change my life. Eventually, while he was still in prison, he filed for divorce because he didn't think we'd have a future.

That was the beginning of the green-card acquisition process. But it wasn't the end. The rest of it was shepherded by the wonderful Cooby family. I was skilled as a domestic, and people knew it. As luck would have it, the Coobys were looking for someone to help the lady of the house with cooking and cleaning. And it was a live-in position. They liked me and hired me. I was honest with them and told them about my immigration status and that I did not yet have a green card. I also told them the Michigan horror story to explain why I was in the United States instead of Canada.

I'd been there for several months when Mr. Cooby asked if I intended to go back to Jamaica to retrieve my five children. My answer was yes. Less than a week later he and his wife offered additional sponsorship—to show I had a job, was stable, and had a network of responsible people I could go to if I ran into difficulty—so I could go get my kids. He even listed their names on the sponsorship documents, making it easier for the immigration officials. I was grateful for his thoughtfulness but had to think about it a little, given the experience I'd had on my way to the United States. I did not want to repeat that, so I asked a lot of questions. I also wanted to know what else I had to do for them while the sponsoring was in progress.

He told me he'd been watching how I did things and loved the way I cared for his wife. He said he wanted to help me. I had no idea at the time how all this would turn out, but I accepted his offer.

Winning my Green Card

Mr. Cooby did everything he said he would. And very soon, he had the papers from Immigration.

I was grateful. He said, "It's okay. Everything will work out and your life will change for the better." And it did. I never had to spend another night in my mother's home or listen to anymore of her nagging or critical comments. In so many ways, it was deliverance for me.

The machinations at Immigration took nine months all told. About one month before the completion of everything, Mr. Cooby's lawyer said I had to go back to Canada to pick up my green card because I'd come from there when I entered the United States.

Oh, Lord. All the memories of my arrival in Toronto, the bad people on the Michigan trip, and the rest came flooding back. You should have seen my face. I asked the attorney if I really had to go back there. He said, "Yes, but you can go to BC instead of Toronto." That was a huge relief, I'll tell you.

Thirty days later, I was on my way to British Columbia, ready to face Immigration again. But this time, my reason for being in Canada was totally different. I was carrying a big envelope of documents that would either help me or deport me. It was up to the authorities.

I hoped and prayed, and thanks to the intercession of my Mr. Cooby—my real sponsor—in a little more than two hours, I went from an illegal alien in Canada to a full-fledged green card holder, a legal American resident.

What a great day that was! I returned to Los Angeles that same night, was met at the airport by my happy boss, and realized I was truly free. Now I had possibilities. There was no more negativity, no more looking over my shoulder in fear I'd be sent back to Jamaica. And, once I'd collected them, my children would have the same opportunities.

I stayed with the Coobys while I filed the papers for my children. I gave them the best service, did everything I could think of for them. They were so pleased they offered to find an apartment for me. They knew I liked going to church and didn't want to hinder that. They also knew I had no car of my own, so they offered to buy me one, not only for transport between home and work, but also so I could take Mrs. Cooby wherever she wanted to go.

My life was better than it ever had been, and I was hugely appreciative of the Coobys' care and kindness. But don't get me wrong. There were challenging moments with my boss and situations with his wife that were unpleasant too. People in Mr. Cooby's social circle objected to me living there and pressured him to let me go. Also, his wife was older, not well, and could be demanding and difficult. She didn't want me to live there or have my kids there, so I moved out to the maid's quarters. But for all that, these people never tried to intimidate me, and I was able to endure. After all, I'd seen tougher times.

CHAPTER 17

I KEEP MY PROMISE

Going after My Kids

ONE MONTH AFTER I RECEIVED my green card, I went back to Jamaica to see my children. My excitement and sense of anticipation was extreme. This was what I'd hoped for! At the same time, though, intuition told me that something might be amiss with my kids, so I couldn't wait for the airplane to touch down.

The Scene at Mrs. Johnson's

Rupert and Lucas met me at the airport. It was my first time in Jamaica since I'd left in 1980. We drove directly to Rupert's aunt's house in the Saint Ann Parish countryside to see my two oldest boys. Her name was Mrs. Johnson. I'd had a strange feeling of unease, which became stronger the closer we got. When we arrived, I stepped up to Mrs. Johnson and asked where my boys were. Rupert looked at me and said, "They're right there in front of you."

What? The two boys standing there were not the children I'd left in this woman's care two years earlier. They looked like African kids you see in documentaries, emaciated and bony. I had a hard time even recognizing them. When I realized they were my boys, I almost died.

Rupert had been sending money and boxes of food to Mrs. Johnson every two weeks, and I'd sent money as well, but she told us she had nothing left. I wondered how Rupert could have been unaware of the situation. He'd visited many times during my absence. How couldn't he have seen the vast change in their appearance? My guess was Rupert realized that if he told me, I'd be on the next plane home, and our plans to leave Jamaica would be destroyed. In addition, at that time, my relationship with Rupert was strained. We'd been apart a long time, we had some issues, he was seeing other women, and I'd become involved with Wayne Thomas, a man I'd met at church in America. *Maybe the thing to do was to leave Rupert here*, I thought.

I was completely shocked by the way my boys looked. "Why are my children like this?" I asked Mrs. Johnson. She replied, "I took care of them and fed them. There is nothing wrong with them." The guilt hit me then, and I was filled with pity for the boys and anger toward this ogress who had starved them.

Meanwhile, the boys were still standing off a piece, staring at me, not running up to hug me or even say hello. They seemed afraid they'd be harmed if they showed any affection. That tore it for me. "Pack their things," I told Mrs. Johnson. "I'm taking the boys with me."

While she was in the house packing, Al and Abdul meekly approached me, and I wrapped my arms around these skeletal children, trying not to crush them. They told me how Mrs. Johnson sent them to school without food and the rest of the time made them eat rotten food left out for days and infested with maggots. The kids had to pluck the maggots aside one by one and force the vile food into their mouths.

They also told me she beat them for no reason and locked them outside in the dark. From my own experience, I knew that was bad—it was pitch black, impossible to see, and who knew what else was out there? The oldest boy clutched his brother's hand, clinging to his only ally these past two years. His eyes seemed to plead, "Don't leave me."

I was beyond furious. When Mrs. Johnson returned and Lucas gathered up the boys' things to put them in his car, he looked at me and said, "Don't ever bring these kids back here." Fat chance of that!

"She's lucky I don't kill her right now," I said, "or chain her up outside in the dark until the critters smell her and come to get their dinner!" I thought that Mrs. Johnson and my mother must have been sisters in a prior life because the same abuse Mama inflicted on me was now being visited upon my children.

I told the boys to say good-bye to Mrs. Johnson because we were leaving. They didn't want to do it. Just before we departed, she looked me and asked, "Aren't you going to thank me?" I responded, "Yes, I'm grateful to you for keeping my kids for two years. For all the evil you've brought down on them, though, I am angry and bitter. So hear this: every time you close your eyes, their faces will be looking at you haunting your sleep. I hope you never have rest or peace until the day you die." And I wasn't kidding.

As things turned out, I was making a prophecy. A couple of years later, she was on her deathbed, cleansing her soul by confessing all the nasty things she'd ever done to anyone. My only regret was my two boys, who to this day remain traumatized by their memories of her, weren't able to hear her pleas for mercy.

I took the two boys from doctor to doctor to get them the help and treatment they needed. All of them said pretty much the same thing—the boys were a little malnourished, but as long as they got plenty of vitamins and healthy food, they'd be fine. I nursed them back to health at Rupert's parents' house.

My oldest daughter was still with my dad and doing fine. Melissa lived with another one of Rupert's aunts and was well cared for. And Junior was with Rupert himself. We hadn't had a big greeting at the airport, because I'd suspected something was wrong with the older boys, so I wanted to get to them first and fast.

A year after that, when Junior was two, I pestered my friend Wayne into traveling to Jamaica and taking Junior back to the United States with him. Wayne did this, despite the tensions between Rupert and me. He even stayed with Rupert while Junior's immigration and travel arrangements were being made.

Creating a Home for My Family

While I was in Jamaica, my grandmother Susan died. It was a hard thing for me to accept because I believed she was the one member of my family who really loved me. She helped me understand why my mother was the way she was, helped and reassured me when I was abused, and told me stories about my father as well. I would miss her dearly.

I stayed an extra week so I could help with the funeral. After that I returned to the United States, again leaving my children but hopefully in better hands. I told them I was only going for a little while and would be back for them soon.

Deep in thought on the airplane, I knew clearly where my priorities lay. When I got back to my employers, I sat down with them and told them I would file for my children at Immigration. I also told them I needed a place of my own so the kids would have a comfortable home. They had no objection. They were happy for me. The immigration process took about five months this time; then, finally, I got the call to retrieve my older boys.

I rented an apartment, moved in, and flew back to Jamaica. When I arrived, I discovered I wasn't prepared for the financial aspect of obtaining a visa, $300 to $400 for each of them. I went to my niece and, thank God, she gave me some of the money I needed. Rupert also gave me money, and a friend who was a church sister paid our airfare back to the United States. Three days later, my two sons and I were on the plane.

Sitting there, a deep feeling of joy and accomplishment came over me. I was keeping my promise to my children. I looked at the two boys, hugged them very tightly, and told them we'd never be parted again.

By then, I was no longer working for the Coobys who had so kindly sponsored me and then gracefully released me. But I still had to support the children and myself, so I found a night nursing job where the kids could accompany me. At other times, a friend watched them.

Six months later, I filed for two more of my children. Immigration officials told me that, because of my income level, I'd only be able to bring one. Disappointed but not discouraged, I flew back to Jamaica to deal with the paperwork.

An Unexpected Complication

When I returned to the United States, I discovered I was pregnant.

This was a serious complication, but there it was. And there were deeper aspects. I still had children in Jamaica who were wondering about their future. Rupert and I had been apart for five years; we'd gone through changes, and issues had surfaced. It looked like there was a possibility Rupert would remain in

Jamaica and disconnect himself from us. Also, during that time, I'd come to depend on Wayne whenever I was unemployed, especially now I had three boys in tow. Wayne generously offered to share his apartment with us. I never saw any bond developing between us, as he had other women and I was still sorting things out with Rupert. But a relationship did happen, and Wayne was the father of this latest child.

All I could say was, "Oh, my God!" This was challenging enough given my circumstances, but I was also waiting for word from Immigration about when I was to collect Melissa. Eight months went by, and I was about ready to give birth, but still no word came. Then, just two weeks before my son Davin was born, I received a letter asking me to go in for an interview. What timing! There was no way I could fly to Jamaica. So Rupert took Melissa in, and a friend who was returning to the United States flew out with her. This happened on the very day I went into labor with my son.

My daughter arrived from Jamaica on October 18, 1983. I didn't see her until two days later, when I came home from the hospital. There I was, with a new baby, four other mouths to feed, and my oldest child Heather still living in Jamaica.

CHAPTER 18

A NEW DAY

Completing Our Family

DESPITE ALL THAT HAD TRANSPIRED, I felt I needed to reach out to Rupert again to determine if there was any way we could reconcile and salvage our union for the sake of the family. I flew down to Jamaica to see him. He said he wanted to move to the United States and asked me to sponsor him for a green card. This time, I said, "No, you'll need to marry me." Well, the happy fact is we did reconcile, and he accepted my pregnancy, and decided he'd raise this new child as his own. Wayne relinquished his rights before Davin was born. Rupert was listed on Davin's birth certificate and became his official father.

On July 4, 1984, I married Rupert, the man I loved, in Jamaica.

We had a beautiful wedding, though few of my family members attended. My father wasn't there; my sister wasn't there. My father thought Rupert was a commoner with poor parents who lived in a shack; he looked down on him and didn't want to dignify the ceremony. They kept my oldest daughter from attending too. The only person from my side was my brother Franklin. He walked me down the aisle and gave me away.

Unfortunately, there was no time for a honeymoon, as I had to return to the United States immediately. To complicate matters, Rupert reported my oldest daughter's father, Erick, was not cooperating and wouldn't sign the immigration papers that would let her leave Jamaica. She couldn't stay there, because she was becoming a young lady, and there was no one to look after her except my father, who was old and sickly.

I had to take matters into my own hands. With my husband and a close friend helping, we got her to the interview with Immigration, which went favorably. Then I flew to Jamaica, gathered her up, and took her back to the United States. Now all six of my children were with me. The only one we were still waiting for was my husband, Rupert.

About six weeks after that, my father passed away. I was unable to return to Jamaica for his funeral because I'd just been there and couldn't afford the airfare again so soon. It made me feel sad, but that's the way it was.

In September 1985, Rupert joined us, and our family was complete. Or so I thought. In January 1987, I gave birth to my seventh child, a son. We named him Triston. This time, both Rupert and I decided enough was enough with the children. We would have no more, so we could give the ones we had a better chance at a decent life.

We lived in Pasadena, California, with seven children. My husband and I worked hard. He worked days, and I worked nights. There were times, I swear, when we passed each other at the door, one coming, one going. On weekends, we slowed down a little, went to church, and spent time with the children and their school activities. In the summer of 1988, we moved to Palmdale, where we helped start a church.

Things went well those first five years my husband was with us. Then, on our fifth anniversary, as we were preparing to renew our marriage vows, my mother announced she was going to marry her common-law man … on our anniversary date. She didn't attend our ceremony, and we didn't go to hers. I did have an encounter with her, though, that gave me flashbacks to the abuse I'd suffered at her hands as a child.

Moving North to Portland

I wanted to get away from those memories and from her, so I asked my husband if we could move. I wanted to go someplace far off, where my mother couldn't come and could communicate only by phone. The problem was the kids were settled in school, on sports teams, and were doing very well. Plus Rupert had a good job.

The question of moving was delayed, though, because I was stricken with viral meningitis and spent two weeks in the hospital. I was told that because of the high fever, I could lose some of my long-term memory and hearing. Luckily I recovered, and neither of those things happened.

About that time, my husband experienced trouble at work, which was very discouraging for him. Though he was performing well, he was demoted, and his job was given to someone else. Besides making me angry, the situation encouraged me to suggest moving to Portland, Oregon. I didn't know why exactly, maybe it was something I read, but Portland seemed like a good place to live and raise our children.

Rupert asked if I knew anyone there. I said, "Only Ethel, a person I met in church, but she can help us find a house." At that, Rupert agreed, and in November 1989, we all boarded our minivan and set out for the Northwest. For the next five days, we looked around, checked neighborhoods, and met people. Most were very friendly and helpful, and they helped us make up our minds. We returned to Palmdale to pack our belongings; then I returned to Portland to find us a house.

It only took me five days. We spent a final Christmas in Palmdale, and on the last day of December 1989, we moved to Portland.

While waiting for the vans to arrive with our furniture, we enrolled the children in school. They began to adapt to their new environment—one in college, one in high school, two in middle school, one in preschool, and the baby home with me. A week later, the trucks came, and we arranged things in our new home.

As we unpacked and placed everything, it finally sunk in that this was home. There was no turning back. Things began to fall into place. The children made connections and new friends, and became involved in school activities. My husband and I enjoyed attending their games—football, basketball, track and field, everything. Truly, the children kept us busy, but we loved every minute.

Both Rupert and I were of the opinion that this was a good place for us. The children had access to things unavailable to them in California. They could *accomplish* here. And it was peaceful for us, at last.

Contact with My Mother

As planned, I'd distanced myself from my mother. After her marriage, she moved with her husband to Oklahoma. I was thankful she'd have her life and I'd have mine. But as a daughter, I felt I had to let her know how we were occasionally. But that was a mistake.

She called back repeatedly, asking to see the children and railing at me for taking them so far away. I was upset but kept my temper. I told her when we were settled in our new home, we could discuss visits. And that was that.

Dealing with Depression

In 1990, I started working as a nursing assistant at a convalescent home. My husband worked evenings, and I worked days. There were reasons for this. One, we had only a single vehicle for transport, and two, one of us had to be home during the day to tend to the youngsters. We didn't hire babysitters; my husband was the babysitter: Mr. Mom during the day, and husband and father the rest of the time. We did what we had to.

The year 1992 turned out to be both the worst and best of times. I was injured in an on-the-job accident at the hospital that caused me to be on and off work for about a year. Eventually I had to be retrained for another position. As a consequence, I suffered from depression. My doctor had prescribed Valium, and one time I took my pill with a drink of alcohol. It was not a good idea at all. I didn't make it far—the middle of the stairs—before I was totally disoriented.

Junior came home from school and called for me. I couldn't answer. He found me on the stairs. He slapped my face and asked, "Mom, what did you take?"

I had the bottle of Valium in my hand. He lifted me and carried me in his arms to my room, then ran to call his dad to come home. He rocked me in his arms and kept asking, with tears in his eyes, "Mom, are you okay? Please don't fall asleep."

My husband was just coming in from work and heard Junior shouting that he need help with me. Rupert jumped into action, bundled me up, put me into the car, and raced to the hospital, where they put me through psychological tests. I was told I was depressed and needed to be on a different kind of medication. All I could think was, *Good thing my son arrived when he did.*

After that ordeal, I'd try to find comfort in my middle daughter, Melissa. I'd get in her bed while she was dressing for school, and we'd talk about simple things, not any particular subject. She had no idea what was going on with me, how fragile I was, but she would listen, and that made me feel better because she wasn't judgmental.

This went on for months, until one day I couldn't stand it anymore. I turned on my husband. I thought I hated him because he'd contributed to my pain. In my sleep, I'd hit him with my fists. This continued, though I had no knowledge of it, until Rupert rebelled and began waking me up. I would go to work, see people that reminded me of my childhood, and I'd have to go to bed for two days. I wouldn't wake up when Rupert shook me. He had to call my job and tell them I was sick. It was awful, and I realized I was losing it.

I told Rupert to take me to the hospital psych unit and leave me there until I was well. He did take me there, but when they examined me, they determined I wasn't a candidate for their program and sent me home again.

My past was coming back to me. I felt like I was in a dark pit, and every time I tried to climb out, someone would step on my hands, making me fall back again. I was screaming inside, but no one could hear me. The voices inside my head kept getting louder and louder. I had to find a way to stop it, so I began a program of psychiatric counseling.

I was in counseling for most of a year, and little seemed to change. Almost in despair, I began attending services at the Church of God. The Holts, the pastor there and his wife, bless them, took me on. They had no idea what they were getting into. I was just a mess, fighting everyone and everything. I was ugly and nasty with people; I let no one near me except the pastor. With good reason, people learned to fear me.

Gradually though, aided by the patient ministrations of the Holts, the horrors of my past began to subside. It became easier to look at myself and deal with other people. And then, at an all-night prayer session, I finally left the pit behind, threw off the stigma of my youth, and emerged into the air and light. It was amazing; I felt like Lazarus, reborn. And the feeling was real. When the meeting was done, I went home, took a bath, ate some breakfast cereal, and went to bed, my husband fast asleep beside me.

I didn't say anything to Rupert, but he immediately saw the change in me. As I did. I knew I'd never be able to repay the pastor, now a bishop, for his love and nurturing at such a critical time. But I thought, maybe he'd be able to find some reward in the fact that I was whole again. And it was time for me to embark on a completely fresh course.

Opening a Jamaican Restaurant

I opened my own Jamaican restaurant in March 1995. I called it Ocho Rios. It was in Portland. This was a joy to me because I loved to cook and knew I could exercise my talent to make people's taste buds tingle with authentic Jamaican food. I was the main cook. We fed people from all walks of life. Any given evening, limousines were parked in our lot. We were featured in newspaper articles from Portland to Miami. We garnered commendations from many different organizations and food critics. A few times, we were even on TV. My older children helped after school and on holidays and weekends when they didn't have sports.

On Saturday nights, bands played Jamaican reggae music. We had it going on.

This arrangement was also more flexible time-wise. I could spend more time with the kids, and my husband helped occasionally in the restaurant. By this time, our youngest was in elementary school.

Things went very well for about six months. Then, one evening during the height of the dinner rush, someone fired a pellet gun through the window, and all our patrons got up and left. That started our downfall. It was hard to convince people they wouldn't be in danger. We hired security people, but that seemed to make the situation worse because people could see them. We struggled on for four more months, but facing big debt if we continued, we closed the restaurant in December.

Another dream shattered and yet another loss, as we had to sell our house and move to Washington in 1997.

Opening Other Things

In 1998, I started a new business, Squeaky Clean Janitorial. I hired two friends to work with me, and we gained a client list quickly. We worked at this successfully for almost two years, at which point I turned the reins over to my employees and went back to work in the medical field as a certified medical assistant.

Then, heading to my job one morning, I was hit by a car and injured. Lord, what next! I was devastated by this turn of events but gritted my teeth and promised myself I wouldn't let anything or anyone put me back into depression. I sang "On Christ the solid rock I stand, all other ground is sinking sand" to keep my spirits up. And I kept moving. With two children still in college, one in high school, and one in elementary school, I had to. My husband was still holding a full-time job, so things were doable.

The very day my youngest left for college in 2005, Rupert and I decided to move back to Portland and pursue yet another interest. This time it was taking care of children less fortunate than my own. And it was revealing work; I found a little of myself in each and every one I took into my home. As of this writing, I'm still doing this. I've fostered fifteen young men so far. Coming into the foster-care program I thought I was going to change lives, but I found out that these young people changed their own. They all had similar stories and similar needs: they wanted a family comprised of a mom and dad. My husband and I were raising children of our own, so we said, "This won't be a problem; we're good at it." We discovered quickly our work was cut out for us because each child is different and each presents different challenges. We had to be Mom and Dad, but in a different way.

Talk about a circle of life. I began as an abandoned, neglected child, and now I'm taking care of other kids who themselves have been abandoned or neglected. I'm thankful I can give back in this way and show others how to endure. It helps me be a better person.

CHAPTER 19

WITH MY MOTHER AS SHE LAY DYING

Some Explanations, Finally

THE DAY MY MOTHER FOUND out she was terminal, I sat at the foot of her bed and looked at her and the doctors. "I'm not going to accept this," I said. I asked her if she wanted treatment. She said no.

"You're just going to die, like that?" I said. "I don't know anything. If you closed your eyes tomorrow, I wouldn't know what to put in your eulogy. I don't know what to say."

She listened to me, and then, with tears in her eyes, she began to tell me her story.

She was born in 1927. She'd had only a fifth-grade education and did odds-and-ends jobs.

My dad lived in Dallas Castle with his wife and family. He worked in Mount James, a few hours away, as a public health inspector. He had a second home there, where he stayed during the workweek, then went home to Dallas Castle on weekends. He was tall, handsome, and rode a white horse with a brown spot on its face. And he was a womanizer.

My mother, about eighteen at the time, worked for my father at the Mount James house as a maid. But he regarded her as more than that. He hated to see other men talk to her because she was pretty. He wouldn't let her out of the house, because men would make passes, and he was jealous. Well, one day he came home drunk and forced himself on her, raped her. It was her first time. She didn't hate him right away, but became very resentful when he fired her because she was pregnant. At that point, she went to live with her mother, and my father began to keep time with someone else.

To prepare for my birth, she went to him to ask for money and support. He refused; he wouldn't give her anything. I was born at 10:00 a.m. on a Sunday morning in November 1949, and the sun was hot at her mother's house in Mount James. She sent word to my father that he now had a daughter, but he denied I was his.

I believe my mother suffered postpartum depression, which later morphed into post-traumatic stress syndrome. She never came out of it until the day she died. She was severely affected mentally and hated the cause of her trauma. Since she couldn't get at my father, she hated me. She didn't want to nurse me or take care of me, so my grandmother took me for the first three months of my life.

That's how old I was that fateful day when she swathed me in a blanket and took me to meet my father at the gate. She argued loudly with him, then set me down on the hilly bank and lunged at him. She was filled with anger when she set me down. I squirmed. My father was sitting on his horse, looking at her scornfully. There was real danger I'd roll off the embankment, so my aunt ran and caught me. My aunt, grandma, mom, and dad were all there. That was when Mom picked me up, handed me to my father, and said, "You have to take her." So he did and left.

He took me to his friend's house, where I was kept for six months. My mother said, "I was told it was one of his girlfriends, and for a good while after that, you were passed around to other girlfriends as well."

Granting Forgiveness

I never heard much from either my mother or my father about the wretched life they gave me as a child. My mother tried to make some amends on her deathbed, but had trouble doing so because she was too far gone.

What I did get from her was that my father took advantage of her, and she became pregnant with me. But he denied I was his child, leaving her to raise me alone, a young woman with little education and no prospects. The only chance for me, she thought, was if she gave me away. She asked around, but nobody wanted me. So she waited until my father came back to the district, and the scene at the gate unfolded. After that, she did what she thought was right: laid me by the side of the road like a dead animal, to be eaten by John crows. Then took me from my aunt's arms and thrust me into my father's, then watched as he took me away.

As she lay there, telling me why she did what she did, I saw tears coursing down her cheeks. I didn't know what she was feeling, but she was clear about one thing: she hated my father for what he'd done to her, and that caused her to hate me as well because I looked so much like him. I was a reminder of her pain.

She said she was sorry and asked me to forgive her. We both began to cry. It was the day after Mother's Day in 2011, and I didn't know what to say to this woman after suffering for sixty-two years of my life. Even though I could understand her position, I was shocked to learn she'd purposefully detested me because of my father's indiscretion. Thinking to myself, *How was any of this my fault?* I hugged her, told her I'd see her the next day, and left. I could feel her eyes on me as I exited the room.

On the way home, I tried to sort through what she'd told me and put it in perspective. *Should I or shouldn't I forgive her and tell her I love her?* Intuition told me I needed to make a decision about this right now; time was running out for both of us.

I went to see her the next day, and took Pastor Holt and Rupert along. As we entered her room, she seemed to be waiting for me. I held her hand. Her eyes were so dim and filmy, it scared me. I looked at her and said, "Mom, please, please forgive me for the things I've done to make you angry, and I'm sorry you're going through this passage from life, but I want you to know God is waiting for you on the other side. I love you." And I meant it.

This was a hugely difficult thing for me to do. But I felt like life and circumstances had given me no choice. It needed to be done.

She said, "I love you, too, daughter. You'll never know how I feel in my heart for you." Then she said, "Please get along with your uncle Vincent. He is my only brother and your only living uncle."

She turned to Pastor Williams, a long-time friend of mine who was also at the hospital, and said, "Please take care of her; she is your sister." And to my husband Rupert, she said, "Please take care of my daughter; she is all yours now."

Rupert replied, "Always."

She said she was tired, which was our cue to leave. I hugged her, kissed her on the cheek, squeezed her hand and said, "If you need me, call, no matter what time." And then we walked away. As we drove off in the car, I felt deep down that would be our final visit.

I was right. The next day, May 11, at 6:15 a.m., I received a call from the caregivers saying, "Your mother is about to take her last breath." I contacted my husband, who'd just left for work, and asked my son to stay with my clients so we could go to her. I didn't realize her passing would affect me so deeply. On the way, I called Pastor Williams to let her know, and she said she'd meet us there. We arrived, and before Rupert could park the car, I jerked the door open and ran to my mother's room.

She was lying in the same position I'd left her. I moved to the bedside, and the sitter who'd been with her all night excused herself. I sat down, took my mother's thin fingers in my hands, and called her name. Her body was still warm. I called her name again, asking her to squeeze my hand if she could hear me. But no, she was gone. She looked so peaceful, I found it sort of a comfort.

A "Royal" Funeral

Pastor Williams arrived and spoke comforting words to Rupert and me. I watched the caregivers position my mother in the bed, then left the room as they cleaned her. I picked out a gown for her to wear to the mortuary.

I was mostly calm as the funeral director, a man from my church, came to take her, but before long my insides began to shake, and I became nauseous. In my mind, I asked my mother, *Shouldn't you have stayed a little longer, so we could talk about these things? Did you have to go so soon?*

Even though the funeral people were gentle and caring, it was hard for me to deal with the paperwork. The process was thorough but impersonal. It made me emotional. I made one request, which they honored—that the gold earrings I'd given her as a Mother's Day gift would be left with her.

When it was time to transfer her body from the bed to a gurney, I broke down. *Oh God, is she really gone?* I thought. *Mama, Mama, I can't take this. It hurts too much!* The sound of the gurney wheels squeaking was alien and gut-wrenching. I passed out on the floor. When I woke up, she was gone. The bed was empty.

Next came the arrangement of her funeral. I've mentioned before how she liked things done up, the royal treatment. Well, she wanted a royal funeral as well, a big church service, then a cremation, with her ashes sprinkled on the river. My mother had a soft spot for fine things because she'd never had any growing up.

She wanted her belongings to be distributed to families in Africa, but told me I should keep her bedroom set for myself because it was her prize possession. That bedroom set, a photo album I have trouble looking at, and an obituary notice are all that remain.

My mother's friends and family came to wish her a final farewell. Pastors Holt and Williams delivered the eulogy, which was sweet and short. They didn't know her, so they were doing it mostly on my behalf, but it was nice. I'd been a congregation member for sixteen years. Something came to me during the service that felt like an epiphany. I didn't do any of this out of guilt or simple respect for the dead, but because it was the right thing for me to do for my mother. In a way, I felt proud of myself. And free.

As for my father, he'd passed many years ago. I have a picture of him on my living room mantle. I look at it sometimes and, in my mind, ask him, *Why did it have to be like this?* I wonder what my life would have been like if he and my mother had raised me in a loving way, even though he was married and had another family.

Not that they ever knew it, but my mother and father got seven beautiful grandchildren and nine great-grandchildren because of me. My mother didn't take the time to embrace them. She stayed out of their lives and blamed me for not initiating contact. At one point she even tried to turn them against me, but it didn't work; they found out the truth for themselves. My father at least tried because for a time my oldest child lived with him.

Finding the Meaning in It All

In retrospect, I can truly say I could not have negotiated this incredible journey alone. God has had a hand in my life since I was conceived, and through every one of my trials, has given me the strength and faith to endure. I made a promise to my children to keep them with me and protect them from harm, and I did it. I made mistakes while raising them, but always got up from those falls and continued on. I came through challenges to my own well-being and sanity with my heart intact. And I married Rupert, the love of my life. To say I'm thankful for these things is the understatement of the era. And they are proof positive to me that, no matter how badly one begins or what troubles one faces along the way, you'll have chances in life to make good in the end, if you believe and don't quit.

CHAPTER 20

IN RETROSPECT

Dedication to My Children

RAISING MY CHILDREN HAS BEEN seriously challenging. At times I felt overwhelmed. I tried to give them what I didn't get when I was young and tried to be a perfect mother when I'd never been taught how. My scars and deficiencies in life were so deep, I worried I couldn't do enough for them. I actually cried out loud in frustration. The Bible says the Holy Spirit makes intersession for us when we don't know what to say, as you can see in Romans 8:26. I used to sing a song called "My hope built on nothing less, than Jesus blood and his righteousness." which would make me feel better.

As I raised these seven kids of mine, feelings of inadequacy (either real or perceived) came along and beat me down inside, creating an unending struggle. I worked hard at every job I had, repeating my childhood experiences when I excelled at home economics and gardening because I couldn't do other academic subjects well.

What I can say now, though, is that each child's face would appear before my eyes and move me to keep going, regardless of cost and circumstance and although I didn't have a manual that explained how to care for each one. I was a ward and a boarder as I grew up, but never anyone's child. I was an orphan who had to utilize examples I saw along the way as references, then try to improve upon them. I did this with all the love I have inside.

Occasionally my kids were angry with me and thought I should have done more for them. They felt abandoned and wondered if I cared enough about them. But I think they know now that I did the best I could. And they are living examples that love is an exchange between people. They are, as they've always been, the beat of my heart.

Experience's Slate

I have had to deal with much emotional turmoil—broken relationships, abandonment, being used and discarded, being let down by people I trusted, having always to find my own path. This, admittedly, has left me with enduring issues. But I'll say this: I've never stopped doing what good I can, regardless of what life has thrown at me. And I no longer look for validation from others; though I do pray daily for guidance, now I look to myself.

Life is like a blank piece of slate. If you don't write on it with a chalk, it stays blank until it breaks and is put aside. But if a piece of old slate is picked up and washed, it still can be marked on. In many ways, that was me. I came into life as a blank slate that was poorly cared for; little of consequence was written on it, so it began to crack apart. But I've kept and used the pieces that are left because much has been required of me. And even though the shards were small and rough, they've served. I am no longer blank. Negative situations have lost their grip on me, and I've taken control of my life. No longer do I try to fit the contents of a quart bottle into a pint.

My children have their own stories to tell. And I'll embrace their opinions, whatever they are. I love all seven dearly. I have regrets about how I handled things in their early years, but I changed course when I felt I was wrong, made amends when necessary, and moved on. I am lifted up and have become strong. Weeping may last for a night, but God's favor and joy comes in the morning and sustains me.

My Children

Meet my babies:

Heather
My first child. She opened motherhood's door for me and was my first true taste of joy and love, although I didn't know how to express it. I understood the mechanics of caring for her, keeping her safe and fed. I left her with my father, Zedekiah, who wanted to raise her while I was at work. I said yes to this arrangement because I knew she would come to no harm and because, as his granddaughter, she would get the nurturing I'd never known. Heather has always been my hope of something better.

Al
My first son. My heart smiled at his birth. Because he always had a rosy disposition, I wanted to hold him constantly. He always made me laugh with his antics. He is our comedian.

Abdul
My skinny, Asian-looking baby. People would tell me how much he looked like Bruce Lee, and they showed so much interest in

him, I realized he was a special child. Abdul was the one I had to fight for, protect, and shield.

Melissa

My beautiful baldheaded baby. She was born with a smile as I delivered her myself at home. We had to wait for the midwife to arrive and separate us. She is a fighter, tough as nails.

Rupert Jr.

He came into the world with a demeanor of leadership. Everything about him made me think he'd be a force. Even as a child, he followed no one, was always about his own business—calm, assured and steadfast.

Davin

My huggy bear. Reserved, cautious and protective, yet a boy who is kind and full of life.

Triston

Our youngest. He is so much like his older brother, Junior, with leadership qualities and the ability to mentor others. His personality is an amalgam of his mom and pop's.

A Little Advice

In the Bible, 1 Peter 5:10 says, "So after you have suffered a while [God] will restore and strengthen you, and he will place you on a firm foundation." I am a living proof of this.

There is no formula for how I got by in life, no recipe to follow, except for some key steps I learned along the way. I'd like to share them, for what they're worth.

One, I cry. It's a natural response when something is wrong. As children, we're often taught to hold back and hide our tears. This is wrong. Tears are cleansing and relieving and precious enough to be stored in a bottle. For me, tears are the words I can't otherwise express. And the path is cleared for answers.

Two, I pray. I believe in God and say so. I always have. Back in the day, I would say the Lord's Prayer over and over. And, as far as I'm concerned, I got a taste of providential power that day at Canadian Immigration. Today, I start each day with thanks, and a request for protection and strength. And I mean it.

Three, I don't stop. I keep moving and doing. It can be hard, and sometimes I don't feel like it. But I press on because I know I must, and in that "must," results are born. I've always believed in and sought after yes, even though I've often been told no. I've viewed every obstacle I've encountered as an agent of clarification, rather than as an enemy. As a consequence, today I'm a fast train that moves forward toward every unfolding opportunity.

In my lifetime, I've sold produce at market, taken fresh fish door to door, been a domestic engineer, worked in the military, run a post office, served as a nurse assistant and lab technician, been a dressmaker, and owned my own business. "I've lived in Jamaica, California and Oregon and have been to Canada and Michigan." I sought out extended education in medical care, languages, and technical skills. I am a jack-of-all-trades and pursue gardening, cooking, sewing, travel, and entertaining with relish. I've always taken interest in helping others and am an active participant at my church. I've also fostered and mentored many children (and I am called Mamma D by most). I share this not to put a feather in my cap, but instead to show the A-to-Z path of my life and survival.

I want to make clear this book is not meant to chastise or belittle anyone, and I am not looking for sympathy. What I'm saying is that no child should have to repeat my experience.

Regardless of how life's journey begins, change and positive direction are possible. Circumstances are not definitive. Everyone has a choice. Any little piece of original slate can be written on again.

But change isn't change until it's a fact and acted upon. The key is to stick with it. I have been made and made myself a wreck in so many ways, but I've never stopped trying to write what my slate never knew during my childhood—love.

And I won't. Ever.

CHAPTER 21

ANOTHER VANTAGE POINT

Melissa's View

VERY FEW PEOPLE HAVE THE courage share their life story, to put it in black and white, for all to see, but that is spirit of the woman I call Mom. Courage is her middle name. My earliest memories of my mom are of her bringing her then five children to the United States to provide them with a better life, education, and experience. She clearly had a vision, one that meant leaving the Jamaica we called home, and going to a foreign land. In sunny California where she landed, she forever changed the trajectory of our lives. This book takes readers on a journey; each page reveals stories of my mom's life as she resurrects the pain of the past to renew her life's purpose in love, family, faith, and business.

It wasn't until my mid-twenties that I truly understood why my mom uprooted us from Jamaica, why our lives there did not fit what she envisioned for her children. Many times over the years, I've listened to my mother speak about her experiences growing up, about her childhood, and about her relationships with members of her family, mainly her father and mother. Often these reveries would leave her unsettled, conflicted, angry, and most certainly sad. As her youngest daughter, I've always considered my mom my hero, my greatest inspiration. She is strong, selfless, generous, ambitious, and absolutely exquisite. However, her pain and sadness were often palpable. It wanted to see her happy but realized she did not know how to be so. Our relationship over the years has had to evolve. It's no secret that mother/daughter dynamics can be challenging and complex, and ours were no different. We fought and argued often, even into my early adult life. At times, friction seemed to rule us.

During my childhood, our household was very strict. My mother and stepfather kept us on a short leash and ruled with an iron fist. I can't say I always felt love in the traditional sense, because our household and lifestyle always seemed so conflicted and stressed. Perhaps we can chalk it up to the fact they were raising seven boisterous children with limited resources. They both worked hard to provide for us, but my mother seemed to be stressed more often. It was clear that love was not spoken; in their minds, it was shown by the fact that they provided a roof over our head, food on the table, and clothes on our backs. But I missed the verbal and physical love my friends received. I knew I was missing something valuable and important. The truth is, I rather would have heard the words "I love you" than have a meal. As a child, I was incapable of understanding why Mommy would go to work and when she came home, all hell would break loose. Often, it seemed like we were the easiest way for her to release her frustration. As a young girl, I certainly was not a perfect child, and I knew if I did something wrong, there'd be consequences. But in our household, the consequences were severe and threatened my self-esteem.

In my teenage years, the lack of love I sensed as a child turned into resentment. But I didn't have the luxury of being resentful toward my mother. I knew my life was calling for me to be better despite my circumstances. For some reason, I was privy to more insight on my mom's life than my siblings were, and it remains that way even today. Growing up, I was often a sounding board for my mom, and I still am. During my teens, I had more responsibility than my siblings too. One memory that stands out is when I was typing my mom's nursing-school homework, which was usually six to ten pages long. I typed every night, sometimes till midnight, for almost a year, on an old manual typewriter; we didn't have access to computers then. When she graduated, I was happier than she was because it meant I could get a little of my life back. The other memory is more painful. When I was in my teens, my mom sometimes came into my room in the middle of the night; I assumed she was sleepwalking. She would wake me up, sit on the edge of the bed, and tell me things that really didn't make sense. I was the only one who experienced this. For months she seemed disoriented at night, stressed, restless, and tormented. Needless to say, between typing her homework and being awakened by her late-night talks, I got very little rest. I still had to go to school, be a good student, pretend I was happy, and smile like my life was normal. The one thing that saved me was sports, which allowed me to focus on myself and my strengths. I felt empowered by the positive relationship and camaraderie I had with my coaches and teammates. Being an athlete changed my life. It was the kind of discipline and support I needed; it built back my self-esteem. I was a good athlete, proud of my accomplishments, and as a result I saw a bit of pride rise in the eyes of my parents for the first time.

I remember well when I heard my mom say, "I love you." I was in my early twenties. It shocked me; I didn't know what to say in return. I assumed this was something we didn't say in our household. But I don't doubt she loved us; she showed it in only way she knew, as a provider and through discipline. I always felt a connection to my mom that was more metaphysical. So a little later on, I started asking her about her childhood, upbringing, experiences, and certainly her relationship with our fathers. Her answers made it clear to me that her childhood, teenage years, and early adulthood were filled with pain, torment, anger, rage, lack of love and abuse. By all accounts, she never had a chance. As I matured and listened to more of her stories, my resentment was transformed into compassion. I started to feel more empathy and hoped my siblings—who were struggling with their own experiences growing up—could find some peace by listening to her. I now know our childhoods affect how we deal with life and people. Unresolved issues and pain have a way to festering, and if they are not dealt with in a healthy way, they can lead to another generation of pain and anguish.

My mom is an excellent cook, and for the longest time, I've wanted her to mass-produce her amazing barbeque sauce, which so many people love. I had a vision of seeing her Mamma D's sauce on shelves everywhere. She made that sauce so many times over the years, she could virtually do it in her sleep. I've encouraged her to start to create a variety of recipes to test, but each time she tried to create the recipe that was once second nature, the sauce didn't taste the same. It was rather unusual for that to happen, but we now know her purpose was not to create another recipe, it was to write this book.

You see, after my grandmother passed away and even during her decline, old hurts and pain from my mom's past raised their ugly heads again. A great deal of my mom's sadness had to do with her mother and their dysfunctional relationship. It spilled over into the parenting of her own children, giving meaning to the notion "you can't give what you never had." I later learned she'd seen had no love from her mother, even though she fiercely desired it. She didn't know anything different until much later in her life. But at that point, we were all grown, reflecting back on our own childhood times. I truly wanted my mother to write this book: one, for her to heal, and two, for her children and grandchildren to know and understand the woman she truly is, that the circumstances of her past do not define who she is today. I am glad she followed through. I encourage her to share her story, so we'll all have a greater understanding of how far she's come. Her story will encourage and inspire not only her children but also many others. Even though she didn't think she could tell it, she absolutely did. And her candor and honesty will free her from the shackles of the past and give my siblings and me permission to do the same.

I am proud of you, Mom!
Your loving daughter,
Melissa R. Hibbért

CHAPTER 22

THE WHEEL

Deloris's Circle of Life

As I cycled through the decision to tell this story and then the effort to remember and relate what actually happened, my whole life often turned into a picture in front of me. And the picture was shaped like a wheel, divided into segments like a pie. The more I thought about it, the more I realized this wheel and its pieces were me—a map of how I've lived and behaved over the years.

{Depiction of Deloris's wheel, a circle cut into eight equal segments, with words in the segments. Starts at bottom left and proceeds counterclockwise. Words in the eight segments: Like, Hate, Forgive, Reconcile, Give up, Move in, Take back, Love.}

Here's how it, and I, work. First, I notice something that interests me, something I like. The attraction encourages me to move closer, find out more, get involved. Second, something awful occurs, and the situation turns truly sour. At this point I may or may not be physically injured, but I'm surely disappointed and discouraged, and I hate it. Third, I discover it's destructive for me to hate, plus it requires energy for which I have other, better uses. So, I find a way to forgive. Fourth, I try to reconcile. Many times the reconciliation happens with the same people I've just forgiven, which sometimes puts me at risk again. Fifth, sure enough, another bad thing comes to pass, assaults my confidence, and prompts me to feel resignation, to give up. But I'm no pushover, so sixth, I move back into the conflict to assert myself and find out what's up. Seventh, moving with some power and purpose, I engage and take back the pieces that are mine, rebuild myself in light of what's gone on, and be me. Eighth, since I have reason now to respect and love myself a little more, I find I can share that love with others again.

That's my circle of life. It's how I roll.

CPSIA information can be obtained at www.ICGtesting.com
Printed in the USA
BVOW07s0427190614

356729BV00001B/3/P